Banking and Financial Markets in India

1947-48 to 2019-20

Banking and Financial Markets in India

1947-48 to 2019-20

Niti Bhasin
Associate Professor, Department of Commerce,
Delhi School of Economics (DSE),
University of Delhi, Delhi

New Century Publications
New Delhi, India

NEW CENTURY PUBLICATIONS
4852 / 24, 1st Floor,
Ansari Road, Daryaganj,
New Delhi – 110 002 (India)

Tel.: 011-4101 7798; 4358 7398; 98112 66355
E-mail: info@newcenturypublications.com

www.newcenturypublications.com

Editorial office:
4800 / 24, Bharat Ram Road,
Ansari Road, Daryaganj,
New Delhi – 110 002

Reprint: 2023

ISBN: **978-81-7708-489-4**

First Published: 2019

Published by New Century Publications and printed at Milan Enterprises, New Delhi.

Designs: Patch Creative Unit, New Delhi.

PRINTED IN INDIA

About the Book

Financial sector is the linchpin of an economic system. A modern economy, characterised by acute specialisation and exchange, is unthinkable without financial intermediaries and financial markets.

After nationalisation of commercial banks in 1969 and 1980, banking business in India was a near-monopoly of the Government of India. Resultantly, banking sector suffered from lack of competition, low capital base, low productivity and high intermediation cost. The role of technology was minimal and the quality of service was poor.

It was in this backdrop, that wide-ranging banking sector reforms in India were introduced as an integral part of the economic reforms process initiated in the early 1990s.

Banking sector reforms have supported the transition of the Indian economy to a higher growth path, while significantly improving the stability of the financial system. In comparison to the pre-reforms period, the Indian banking system today is more stable and efficient.

Information technology (IT) has transformed the functioning of banking business. Banks are using electronic and telecommunication networks for delivering a wide range of value added products and services.

Financial markets in India have seen considerable development since financial sector reforms were initiated in the 1990s. The process of transition in respect of all financial market segments has been largely disruption-free, accommodating the unique features of the existing system while trying to align with the best international practices.

Prior to the onset of financial sector reforms in 1991, the capital market structure in India was subject to several controls and opaque procedures. Indian capital market has witnessed a series of reforms since the early 1990s.

This book traces developments in the banking sector and financial markets in India since Independence in 1947.

About the Author

Dr. Niti Bhasin is presently Associate Professor in the Department of Commerce, Delhi School of Economics (DSE), University of Delhi, Delhi. A gold medallist in the M. Com. examination of 2000 of University of Delhi, she holds M.Phil. and Ph.D. degrees from the Department of Commerce, University of Delhi. She has published research papers in refereed academic journals including *Multinational Business Review* (Emerald), *Journal of International Trade and Economic Development* (Taylor and Francis), and *Global Business Review* (Sage).

Dr. Bhasin has attended and presented papers at various international conferences/seminars including the Third World Finance Conference, Rio de Janeiro (Brazil), 2012; Mahidol University, Bangkok (Thailand), 2016; and Henley Business School, University of Reading, London (UK), 2017. She is the recipient of Best Business Academic of the Year Award (2011) by Indian Commerce Association. Before joining the Department of Commerce, Delhi School of Economics, she taught for about 4 years at Shri Ram College of Commerce (SRCC), University of Delhi. Her areas of specialisation include international business, foreign investment, finance and taxation.

Contents

Preface

Banking sector is at the heart of an economic system. A modern economy, characterised by acute specialisation and exchange, is unthinkable without financial intermediaries. India has a long and chequered history of financial intermediation, particularly commercial banking.

Soon after Independence in 1947, Government of India followed a policy of social control of important financial institutions. The nationalisation of the Reserve Bank of India (RBI) in 1948 marked the beginning of this policy. This was followed by the takeover of the then Imperial Bank of India in 1956 which was rechristened as State Bank of India. In another significant development, Government nationalised 14 major commercial banks in 1969. In 1980, 6 more commercial banks were nationalized and brought under public ownership.

Thus, till the initiation of economic reforms in early 1990s, banking business in India was a near-monopoly of the Government of India. The underlying philosophy of this approach was to encourage growth—via availability of adequate credit at reasonable and concessional rates of interest—in areas where commercial considerations did not allow for disbursal of credit.

Nationalisation of commercial banks in 1969 and 1980 was a mixed blessing. After nationalisation there was a shift of emphasis from industry to agriculture. The country witnessed rapid expansion in bank branches, even in rural areas. However, bank nationalisation created its own problems like excessive bureaucratisation, red-tapism and disruptive tactics of trade unions of bank employees.

Being a near-monopoly of the Government, the banking sector suffered from lack of competition, low capital base, low productivity and high intermediation cost. The role of technology was minimal and the quality of service was not given adequate importance. Banks also did not follow proper risk management systems and the prudential standards were weak. All these resulted in poor asset quality and low profitability.

It was in this backdrop, that wide-ranging banking sector reforms in India were introduced as an integral part of the economic reforms process initiated in the early 1990s.

Banking sector reforms have supported the transition of the Indian economy to a higher growth path, while significantly improving the stability of the financial system. In comparison of the pre-reforms period, the Indian banking system today is more stable and efficient. However, these gains need to be consolidated, so that these could be translated to drive the institutions, markets and practices into a mature financial system that can meet the challenges of sustaining India on a higher growth trajectory.

Information technology (IT) has transformed the functioning of businesses, the world over. Banks have traditionally been in the forefront of harnessing technology to improve their products, services and efficiency. They have, over a long time, been using electronic and telecommunication networks for delivering a wide range of value added products and services. The delivery channels include, inter alia, direct dial-up connections, private networks, public networks and the devices including telephone, personal computers (PCs), automated teller machines (ATMs), networking of ATMs in the form of shared payment networks, and core banking solutions.

Electronic banking (e-banking) is a generic term encompassing internet banking, telephone banking, mobile banking etc. In other words, it is a process of delivery of banking services and products through electronic channels such as satellite, telephone, internet, cell phone etc. The concept and scope of e-banking is still evolving. Internet banking is a major component of e-banking.

Internet banking offers different online services like balance enquiry, requests for cheque books, recording stop-payment instructions, balance transfer instructions, account opening and other forms of traditional banking services. These are mostly traditional services offered through internet as a new delivery channel. Banks are also offering payment services on behalf of their customers who shop in different e-shops, e-malls etc.

Developments in mobile telephony, as also the mobile phone density in the India, present a unique opportunity to leverage the mobile platform to meet the objectives and challenges of financial inclusion. By harnessing the potential of mobile technology, large sections of the un-banked and under-banked society can be empowered to become inclusive through the use of electronic banking services.

Financial markets in India have seen considerable development since financial sector reforms were initiated in the 1990s. Given the imperatives of the prevailing context, the initial nudge had to be provided through specific policy instruments and actions, but over a period of time these markets have acquired a dynamic of their own. The process of transition in respect of all financial market segments has been largely disruption-free, accommodating the unique features of the existing system while trying to align with the best international practices.

Prior to the onset of financial sector reforms in 1991, the capital market structure in India was subject to several controls and opaque procedures. The objective of control over capital issues was to channel the limited capital resources available for investment in the country into desired areas.

Indian capital market has witnessed a series of reforms since the early 1990s. These reforms have been implemented in a gradual and sequential manner, based on international best practices and modified to suit the needs of the country.

Reforms in the capital market have had a multi-dimensional impact. The significance of the capital market has improved in providing a mechanism for allocation of resources as is reflected in increase in its share in the sources of finance for the corporates.

Acknowledgements

This work draws, in part, on the information provided in the publications and websites of various national and international institutions/organizations, in particular the Ministry of Finance, Government of India, Ministry of Corporate Affairs, Government of India, Reserve Bank of India (RBI), Securities and Exchange Board of India (SEBI), National Bank for Agriculture and Rural Development (NABARD), World Bank, International Monetary Fund (IMF), and Bank for International Settlements (BIS). Use of information from these sources is gratefully acknowledged.

New Delhi **Niti Bhasin**

Part I
Financial Sector Reforms in India

1

Financial Sector in the Pre-reforms Period: 1947-1990

At the time of Independence in 1947, India had a fairly well-developed banking system. The process of financial development in independent India has hinged effectively on the development of commercial banking, with impetus given to industrialisation based on the initiatives provided in the five year plans.

Soon after Independence in 1947, Government of India followed a policy of social control of important financial institutions. The nationalisation of the Reserve Bank of India (RBI) in 1948 marked the beginning of this policy. This was followed by the takeover of the then Imperial Bank of India in 1955 which was rechristened as State Bank of India. In 1956, 245 life insurance companies were nationalised and merged into the newly created Life Insurance Corporation of India (LIC). In another significant development, Government nationalised 14 major commercial banks in 1969. The year 1972 saw the nationalisation of general insurance companies and the setting up of General Insurance Corporation (GIC). In 1980, 6 more commercial banks were nationalized and brought under public ownership.

Trade and industrial activities during the 1950s, and the 1960s reflected the dominance of banking as the critical source. The number of banks and branches had gone up, notwithstanding the consolidation of small banks, and the support given to the community-operative credit movement. Functionally, banks catered to the needs of the organised industrial and trading sectors. The primary sector consisting of agriculture, forestry, and fishing had to depend largely on their own financing and on sources outside the commercial banks.

The course of development of financial institutions and

markets during the post-Independence period has been largely guided by the process of planned development pursued in India with emphasis on mobilisation of savings and channelising investment to meet Plan priorities. The adoption of bank-dominated financial development strategy was aimed at meeting the sectoral credit needs, particularly of agriculture and industry. Towards this end, the RBI (nationalised in 1948) concentrated on regulating and developing mechanisms for institution building. The commercial banking network was expanded to cater to the requirements of general banking and for meeting the short-term working capital requirements of industry and agriculture. Specialised development finance institutions (DFIs) with majority ownership of the RBI were set up to meet the long-term financing requirements of industry and agriculture. To facilitate the growth of these institutions, a mechanism to provide concessional finance to these institutions was also put in place by the RBI.

1.1 Nationalisation of Imperial Bank of India (1955)

Soon after Independence, India launched its First Five Year Plan (1951-56). The Plan accorded high priority to the development of rural India, particularly agriculture. The All India Rural Credit Survey Committee recommended the creation of a State-partnered and State-sponsored bank by taking over the Imperial Bank of India and integrating with it the former State-owned or State-associated banks. Accordingly, an Act was passed in the Parliament in May 1955 and the State Bank of India was constituted on July 1, 1955. Later, the State Bank of India (Subsidiary Banks) Act was passed in 1959 enabling the State Bank of India to take over eight former State-associated banks as its subsidiaries.

1.2 Nationalisation of Life Insurance Business (1956)

By the Life Insurance (Emergency Provisions) Ordinance, 1956, promulgated by the President of India on January 19, 1956, the management and control of life insurance business in

India, including the foreign business of Indian insurers, and the Indian business of foreign insurers, vested with immediate effect in the Central Government. With this the life insurance business passed from the private sector to the public sector. This was a step never before attempted any where in the world on such a large scale.

Though the Ordinance was promulgated in January 1956, the Life Insurance Corporation Act was passed in the next session of parliament. According to this Act the Life Insurance Corporation of India came into existence on September 1, 1956.

1.3 Nationalisation of Commercial Banks (1969 and 1980)

The process of state domination of financial sector was given impetus with the adoption of the policy of social control over banks in 1967, reinforced in 1969 by the nationalisation of 14 major scheduled commercial banks. In April 1980, government nationalised 6 more commercial banks. Driven largely by public sector initiative and policy activism, commercial banks have a dominant share in total financial assets and are the main source of financing for the private corporate sector. They also channel a sizeable share of household savings to the public sector. Besides, in recent years, they have been performing most of the payment system functions. With increased diversification in recent years, banks in both public and private sectors have been providing a wide range of financial services.

1.4 Nationalisation of General Insurance Business (1973)

The general insurance business was nationalized with effect from January 1, 1973, through the General Insurance Business (Nationalization) Act, 1972. However, as a prelude to the above Act, the Government took over the management of all the operating companies in 1971 through General Insurance (Emergency Provision) Act, 1971. The emergency Act provided for the appointment of custodians who were empowered to exercise control over these companies subject to the directions of the Central Government.

At the time of nationalization of these companies, there were a total of 107 companies underwriting general insurance business in India. All these companies were amalgamated and grouped into four, namely the National Insurance Company Limited, the New India Assurance Company Limited, the Oriental Insurance Company Limited, and the United India Insurance Company Limited with head offices at Kolkata, Mumbai, Delhi and Chennai respectively. The General Insurance Company (GIC) was formed as a holding company in November 1972. The GIC was constituted for the purpose of superintending, controlling and carrying out the business of general insurance. The entire capital of GIC was subscribed by the Government and that of four companies by the GIC on behalf of the Government of India.

Broadly speaking, financial development in India up to the early 1990s was, by and large, a state-induced activity.

1.5 Rethinking on State Domination of Financial Sector

Nationalisation of commercial banks in 1969 and 1980 was a mixed blessing. After nationalisation there was a shift of emphasis from industry to agriculture. The country witnessed rapid expansion in bank branches, even in rural areas. However, bank nationalisation created its own problems like excessive bureaucratisation, red-tapism and disruptive tactics of trade unions of bank employees.

Being a near-monopoly of the Government, the banking sector suffered from lack of competition, low capital base, low productivity and high intermediation cost. The role of technology was minimal and the quality of service was not given adequate importance. Banks also did not follow proper risk management systems and the prudential standards were weak. All these resulted in poor asset quality and low profitability.

Among non-banking financial intermediaries, development finance institutions (DFIs) operated in an over-protected environment with most of the funding coming from assured sources at concessional terms.

The mutual fund industry also suffered from lack of competition and was dominated for long by one institution, viz. the Unit Trust of India (UTI).

Non-banking financial companies (NBFCs) grew rapidly, but there was no regulation regarding their asset side. Financial markets were characterised by control over pricing of financial assets, barriers to entry, high transaction costs and restrictions in movement of funds between the market segments. This, apart from inhibiting the development of the markets, also affected their efficiency.

Similarly, capital market structure in India was subject to several controls and opaque procedures. The trading and settlement system was outdated and not in tune with international practices. Raising of capital from the market was regulated by the Capital Issues (Control) Act, 1947 which was administered by the Controller of Capital Issues (CCIs) in the Ministry of Finance, Government of India. The scheme of controls under the Act required all the companies to obtain prior consent for issues of capital to the public. Pricing as well as the features of the capital structure (such as debt-equity ratios), were controlled by the Government.

Securities Contracts (Regulation) Act was administered by the Directorate of Stock Exchanges also in the Ministry of Finance. It empowered the Government to recognise/derecognise stock exchanges, stipulate rules and bye-laws for their functioning, compel listing of securities by public companies etc. Such a system of regulation and control was fragmented and inadequate in the context of liberalisation wave sweeping across the world. Urgent measures were needed to relax controls and modernise the functioning of capital market.

Furthermore, state monopoly of insurance business resulted in limited availability of insurance products, lack of information technology and poor quality of insurance services. In this connection, the Committee on Reforms in Insurance Sector (Chairman: R.N. Malhotra), which was set up in April 1993 and which submitted its report in January 1994, remarked,

- "Indian insurance industry lacks depth, diversity and reach, both geographically as well as in terms of insurable population, as there was immensely vast potential yet to be tapped;
- It provides poor customer service in terms of pricing, adequacy and appropriateness of covers and the much needed and timely claims settlement;
- It lacks the global dimensions having remained in isolation too long".

In fact, the environment in the financial sector till the initiation of reforms in 1991 was not particularly conducive for the development of deep and wide financial markets. In fact, it had resulted in segmented and underdeveloped markets characterised by paucity of instruments, and limited number of participants. Banks and financial institutions functioned in a highly regulated environment, characterised by an administered interest rate structure, quantitative restrictions on credit flows, fairly high reserve requirements and pre-emption of significant proportion of lendable resources for the priority and Government sectors.

While the quantitative restrictions resulted in credit rationing for the private sector, interest rate controls led to suboptimal use of credit resulting in low levels of investment and growth. These, coupled with other factors such as the absence of proper accounting, transparency and prudential norms, resulted in a large build-up of non-performing assets in the banking system. All this led to erosion of profitability in the banking sector, besides decline in productivity and efficiency. The bank-based and highly controlled regime turned out to be inimical to financial market development.

Thus, until the early 1990s, the role of the financial system in India was primarily restricted to the function of channelling resources from surplus to deficit sectors. Whereas the financial system performed this role reasonably well, its operations came to be marked by some serious deficiencies over the years. The Indian Government determined the quantum, allocation and the price of credit, a situation referred to as *financial repression* by some experts.

It was in this backdrop, that wide-ranging financial sector reforms in India were introduced as an integral part of the economic reforms initiated in the early 1990s.

2

Financial Sector in the Post-reforms Period: Since 1991

A safe and sound financial sector is a pre-requisite for sustained growth of any economy. Globalisation, deregulation and advances in information technology in recent years have brought about significant changes in the operating environment for banks and other financial institutions. These institutions are faced with increased competitive pressures and changing customer demands. These, in turn, have engendered a rapid increase in product innovations and changes in business strategies.

Considering the strategic importance of the financial sector, the Government of India set up a Committee on Financial System (Chairman: M. Narasimham) in 1991. It was asked to examine all aspects relating to the structure, organisation, functions and procedures of the Indian financial system. The Committee submitted its report in November 1991. It was presented to Parliament in December 1991. The report focussed mainly on enabling and strengthening measures for the financial sector.

The Committee on Banking Sector Reforms (Chairman: M. Narasimham), 1998 placed greater emphasis on structural measures and improvement in standards of disclosure and levels of transparency in order to align the Indian standards with international best practices. Pursuant to the recommendations of the two Committees, financial reforms introduced in India have brought about considerable improvements as reflected in various parameters relating to capital adequacy, asset quality, profitability and operational efficiency.

2.1 Focus of Financial Sector Reforms

Financial sector reforms have focused on the following.

1. Elimination of segmentation across various markets in order to facilitate transmission of impulses across markets.
2. Easing the liquidity management process.
3. Making resource allocation more efficient across the economy.

For above purposes, restrictions on pricing of assets have been removed and new instruments introduced. Technological infrastructure has been strengthened. Liberalisation of the financial sector has included, among others, the following measures.

1. Deregulation of interest rates.
2. Introduction of new products.
3. Lowering of restrictions on specialisation/diversification of banks.
4. Emergence of new institutions such as primary dealers and mutual funds.
5. Withdrawal of reserve requirements on inter-bank borrowings.
6. Withdrawal of credit controls and excessively high reserve requirements.
7. Deregulation and development of markets.
8. Moves toward privatisation of financial services.
9. Easing of restrictions in respect of banks' foreign currency investments.

These reforms have paved the way for integration among various segments of the financial system. It is widely accepted that reduction/removal of financial repression has enhanced the efficiency and potential growth of the Indian economy.

2.1.1 Banking Sector Reforms: The key objective of reforms in the banking sector has been to enhance the stability and efficiency of banks. To achieve this objective, various reform measures were initiated that could be categorised broadly into three main groups: (a) enabling measures, (b) strengthening measures, and (c) institutional measures.

Enabling measures were designed to create an environment where banks could respond optimally to market signals on the basis of commercial considerations. Salient among these included reduction in statutory pre-emptions so as to release greater funds for commercial lending, interest rate deregulation to enable price discovery, granting of operational autonomy to banks and liberalisation of the entry norms for financial intermediaries.

The strengthening measures aimed at reducing the vulnerability of banks in the face of fluctuations in the economic environment. These included, *inter alia*, capital adequacy, income recognition, asset classification and provisioning norms, exposure norms, improved levels of transparency, and disclosure standards.

Institutional measures focused on reforms in the legal framework pertaining to banks and creation of new institutions.

2.2 India's Approach to Financial Sector Reforms

Financial sector reforms in India have formed an important component of the overall economic reforms process initiated in the early 1990s. These reforms have followed a well calibrated approach.

The general approach to financial sector reforms has been a transparent, collaborative and consultative process aimed at resolving many possible dilemmas. The reform process itself was characterised by caution with a tilt towards preserving stability, careful sequencing of measures, mutually reinforcing monetary measures and ensuring consistency and complementarity with other policies.

Further, reforms in the financial markets have been undertaken within the overall monetary policy framework and in co-ordination with reforms in the money and foreign exchange markets. Many of the major reforms have been implemented in phases, allowing for transition so as not to destabilise market conditions or any group of participants or the financial system in general.

In the context of maximising benefits of financial integration and minimising the risks, the link with the real sector cannot be ignored. In India, reforms in the financial sector started early in the reform cycle which imparted efficiency and stability to the real sector. The financial sector can add competitive strength and growth if reforms in the financial and real sectors keep apace. A major agenda for reform at this juncture for India, given the impressive all-round confidence in the economy, relates to the structure and functioning of institutions and in particular lowering the high transaction costs prevalent in the system. There are several dimensions to the transaction costs—ranging from legal provisions, the judicial system and procedures to attitudes.

The policy of gradualism that has been followed by India focuses on evolution of appropriate institutional framework and the sequencing of reforms based on the experience gained so far. The sequencing and pace of reforms are also vital to safeguard monetary and financial stability and avoid reversals. The issues in this context include: (a) whether bank-based or market-based system of development should be adopted, (b) order of sequencing of reforms of various segments of the financial market to be followed, and (c) whether or not capital account liberalisation should precede domestic financial market reform.

2.2.1 Gradualist Approach: By following a gradualist approach, India has successfully avoided financial disasters as were experienced by some East Asian countries. A number of developing countries especially in Asia that moved early on to the path of economic liberalization had experienced large capital inflows through the 1980s and the first half of the 1990s. Large capital inflows, however, carried the risk of financial sector vulnerability, where the use of such flows is not regulated by application of appropriate mix of macroeconomic and structural policy measures. The recent currency and financial crises in Mexico and Thailand, followed by Korea and Indonesia, provide many insights about the problems that would arise when exchange rates are inflexible, and banking and financial systems are weak.

The experience of the crisis-affected countries highlights the need for setting in place regulatory and supervisory frameworks to ensure the safety and stability of financial systems. Their experience also underscored the premise that financial development is only a necessary condition for sustainable growth, and by no means sufficient. In fact, with the incidence of the costs of financial crisis falling on the sovereign governments, financial stability has come to occupy a centre-stage in public policy making along with the requirement of ensuring that the efficiency of the financial sector is high.

Implementation of the reforms process has had several unique features. Financial sector reforms were undertaken early in the reform cycle. Notably, the reforms process was not driven by any banking crisis, nor was it the outcome of any external support package. Besides, the design of the reforms was crafted through domestic expertise, taking on board the international experiences in this respect. The reforms were carefully sequenced with respect to the instruments to be used and the objectives to be achieved.

Thus, prudential norms and supervisory strengthening were introduced early in the reform cycle, followed by interest-rate deregulation and a gradual lowering of statutory pre-emptions. The more complex aspects of legal and accounting measures were ushered in subsequently when the basic tenets of the reforms were already in place.

2.3 Strategy of Financial Sector Reforms

Reforms in the financial sector are wide-ranging, encompassing institutional, legal and technological aspects of the functioning of financial intermediaries and financial markets.

2.3.1 Strengthening Financial Infrastructure: Measures to improve market infrastructure must be implemented at an early stage of reform alongside appropriate legal framework. These conditions facilitate growth of financial transactions including inter-bank transactions and active liquidity management.

Presence of well-established institutions, soundness of bank balance sheets, existence of adequate safety nets and vigilant supervision are the pre-requisites for successful financial liberalisation. The reform process in India within the banking system has sought to strengthen the balance sheets of individual banks, empower banks to respond in the most optimal manner to market stimuli and to establish institutions to ensure a level playing field for all market participants and provide a back-up system for contingencies.

Competition has been infused into the financial system by licensing new private banks since 1993. Foreign banks have also been given more liberal entry.

Progress has also been generated through demonstration and spread effects of advanced technology and risk management practices accompanying new private banks and foreign banks. Given the fiscal constraint being faced by the Government and in keeping with the evolving principles of corporate governance, the Government permitted public sector banks to raise fresh equity from markets to meet their capital shortfalls or to expand their lending. Several public and private sector banks have accessed the domestic equity market. Public sector banks have also raised capital through GDRs/ADRs while many banks have raised subordinated debt through the private placement route.

2.3.2 Financial Regulation and Supervision: The quality of financial regulation and supervision as well as of information and the legal system are important for reaping the benefits of globalisation. Hence, enactment of enabling legislation has been a priority area of the reforms. The Board for Financial Supervision (BFS) was constituted in 1994, with the mandate to exercise the powers of supervision and inspection in relation to the banking companies, financial institutions and non-banking financial companies.

With the switchover to international best practices on income recognition, asset classification and provisioning, the problem of non-performing assets (NPAs) assumed critical importance. It was widely perceived that the level of NPAs in India was high by international standards. The problem needed to be tackled urgently and from different fronts. A menu approach has been adopted to tackle this major constraint confronting the banking sector. These policy measures have resulted in reduction in gross NPAs in the banking system.

The need for monitoring and supervising becomes even more important systemically with the opening up of the economy. Thus, the prudential regulations were fortified by reorientation of *on-site inspections* and introduction of *off-site surveillance*. The focus of inspection has shifted from ensuring appropriate credit planning and credit allocation under a closed economy framework to assessment of the bank's safety and soundness and to identify areas where corrective action is needed to strengthen the institution and improve its performance.

In view of the growing liberalisation of the external sector and international banking by banks in India, monitoring of the cross-border flow of funds has assumed importance. RBI now compiles and disseminates international banking statistics (IBS) on the lines of the reporting system devised by the Bank for International Settlements (BIS). The locational banking statistics (LBS) provide the gross position of international assets and international liabilities of all banking offices located in India. They report exclusively banks' international transactions including the transactions with any of their own branches/subsidiaries/joint ventures located outside India.

2.3.3 Financial Openness: In India, opening up of the financial sector in terms of entry of foreign entities and easing of restrictions on international transactions took place within the broader process of reforms. The constant policy concern in this respect has been that of preparing the financial sector for global competition and taking preventive measures for the potential vulnerabilities that it might engender.

Despite their extensive branch network, the biggest banks in India are miniscule compared to most of the multinational banks, in terms of standard parameters like assets or deposits. Hence, the initial focus of reforms in the financial sector was to strengthen the domestic financial infrastructure, make it more competitive and to provide banks greater freedom in their foreign operations.

Since 1991, the presence of foreign entities within the Indian banking sector has increased and so also the international transactions of Indian banks.

International experience has shown that the cost of financial intermediation declines and quality of financial services improves with opening of the economy. However, openness should be preceded by deregulation and strengthening of institutional framework in order to limit contagious influences. The strategy adopted in India has been to maximise the beneficial effects of openness while minimising the adverse consequences. Financial crisis due to internal/external factors have been averted, while the financial system has been progressively deregulated and strengthened.

In short, India's financial sector has made rapid strides in reforming itself and aligning itself to the new competitive business environment. While the operational and supervisory practices in the sector have progressively approximated international best practices, the process of convergence is not yet complete. Greater conformity to prudential norms of international standards as also adoption of better systems of risk management will enhance the stability of the financial system even as banks expand the range and volume of their operations.

2.4 International Security Standards

There are at present a number of security standards available for different financial applications. Most of them are internationally accepted and part of the ISO standards. These international standards such as the BS7799 [1] have been accepted by the RBI. Banks, however, could also put in place measures which conform to their own policies and ensure regular and periodical audit.

The objectives of these standards are as listed below.

1. To provide management direction and support for information security which is a basic pre-requisite for BS7799.
2. To manage information security within the organisation, maintain the security of organisational information processing facilities and information assets accessed by third parties, and to maintain the security of information when the responsibility for information processing has been outsourced to another organisation.
3. To maintain appropriate protection of corporate assets and ensure that information assets receive an appropriate level of protection.
4. To reduce risks of human error, theft, fraud or misuse of facilities and minimise the damage from security incidents and malfunctions and learn from such incidents.
5. To ensure the correct and secure operation of information processing facilities, minimise the risk of systems failures, to protect the integrity of software and information and maintain the integrity and availability of information processing and communication.
6. To control access to information, prevent unauthorised access, detect unauthorised activities and ensure information security when using mobile computing and tele-networking facilities.
7. To ensure security is built into operational systems, to prevent loss, modification or misuse of user data in application systems.
8. To counteract interruptions to business activities and critical business processes from the effects of major failures or disasters.
9. To prevent breaches of any criminal or civil law, statutory, regulatory or contractual obligations and of any security requirements, ensure compliance of systems with organisational security policies and standards and minimise interference to/from the system audit process.

2.5 Accounting and Auditing Standards

Indian accounting standards are generally in alignment with international accounting standards, except for some modifications to suit local customs, usages and level of development in the country. There has been significant progress in accounting standards though some issues remain to be addressed. There are suggestions that Institute of Chartered Accountants of India (ICAI) needs to be made an autonomous body with its own staff and independent funding. Need has also been felt to develop country-specific/sector-specific standards where similar standards are not developed by International Accounting Standards Board (IASB). Similarly, ICAI should make attempts to attain convergence with International Financial Reporting Standards (IFRS).

India is one of the earliest countries to have adopted International Standards on Auditing by amending them to suit Indian requirements. There has been significant progress since ROSC-2004. However, there are some areas which need attention. Auditing and Assurance Standards Board (AASB) needs to take steps to attain convergence with International Standards on Auditing. It needs to take proactive steps by bringing out more technical guidance and other literature to help small and medium practitioners to understand standards. There is a need to give functional independence to AASB.

2.5.1 Marking-to-market: The Indian accounting standards are generally aligned to the International Financial Reporting Standards, though there are some differences. India is yet to fully adopt the marking-to-market requirements as available in the international standards. The Indian standards are relatively conservative and do not permit recognition of unrealised gains in the profit and loss account or equity, though unrealised losses are required to be accounted. Banks are required to mark-to-market the investments in the held for trading (HFT) and available for sale (AFS) categories at periodical intervals, on a portfolio basis, and provide for the net losses and ignore the net gains.

This has proved to be a stabilising factor, inasmuch as it has not induced an imbalance in the incentive structures and has also proved to be less pro-cyclical.

2.6 Technological Solutions for Financial Services

Most of the initiatives regarding technology are aimed at providing better and more efficient customer service by offering multiple options to the customer. The death of distance, which is a by-product of technology, has become a reality in the banking sector. Technology is also playing a key role in banks' strategy for gaining a competitive edge.

Many banks have commenced the process of setting up core banking solutions, which are at various stages of implementation. While such systems are already in place in respect of new private sector banks, a few old private sector banks and public sector banks are also quickly moving to set up such processes. This would benefit the customer in the banking sector. Computerisation of the business of banks has been receiving high importance. The public sector banks have already achieved a high level of computerisation of their business. The directive from the Central Vigilance Commission (CVC) to achieve 100 percent computerisation has resulted in renewed vigour towards computerisation of branches.

Networking has been receiving focused attention by banks. This activity is also being monitored by the RBI. Most banks have their own corporate networks to facilitate inter-branch and branch-controlling office communication in an electronic mode. Inter-bank and inter-city communication takes place through the Indian Financial Network (INFINET). As part of the INFINET, the terrestrial lines have been augmented to provide for increased data transfer capabilities. All these have resulted in the dependence of banks on network-based computing which has benefited the customer.

INFINET also provides for safe and secure transmission of electronic messages with the use of public key infrastructure (PKI) which has the legal backing of Information Technology

Act, 2000. It also provides for messages to flow in a structured environment, using the structured financial messaging solutions (SFMS), which provides for inter-operability of messages so that straight through processing (STP) is achieved.

Another major development witnessed in recent years is the growth in multiple delivery channels to customers such as internet-based banking, mobile banking and anywhere banking. This has benefited the customers and the banks alike. While customers have now a wide variety of options to choose from, banks have been able to reduce costs which have had a positive impact on their profitability.

These developments have, however, also posed certain challenges. In a world where geographical barriers are losing significance, it is essential that security is given prime importance in a transnational scenario where large sums of money are at stake. While the challenges relating to physical security could be confronted with relative ease, the position is much more complicated in respect of IT security. The RBI has, therefore, provided guidelines on information system (IS) security as also IS audit which banks can use for their benefit. These are generic in nature and do not have any prescriptive tones.

2.7 Global Financial Crisis and India's Financial Sector

Beginning mid-September 2008, the Indian financial markets came under pressure owing to the knock-on effects of the global crisis through the monetary, financial, real and confidence channels. The contagion was initially felt in the equity markets due to the reversal of foreign institutional portfolio flows. With sharp tightening of global liquidity, Indian banks and corporates saw their overseas financing drying up. As a means of substitute financing, corporates withdrew their investments from domestic money market mutual funds, thereby putting redemption pressure on them and on NBFCs where the mutual funds had invested a significant portion of their funds. This substitution of overseas financing by domestic financing brought both money market and credit market under pressure.

Moreover, the foreign exchange market was impacted by the reversal of capital flows as part of the global de-leveraging process. Simultaneously, corporates were converting the funds raised locally into foreign currency to meet their external obligations. Both these factors put downward pressure on the rupee. In the foreign exchange market, the Indian rupee generally depreciated against major currencies. In the credit market, the lending rates of scheduled commercial banks (SCBs) have begun to exhibit some moderation since November 2008.

In response, RBI initiated several measures since September 16, 2008 to augment domestic and foreign exchange liquidity for proper functioning of the domestic markets and maintaining financial stability. While the overall policy approach has been able to mitigate the potential impact of the turmoil on domestic financial markets and the economy, with the increasing integration of the Indian economy and its financial markets with rest of the world, there is recognition that the country does face some downside risks from these international developments.

The risks arise mainly from the potential reversal of capital flows on a sustained medium-term basis from the projected slow down of the global economy, particularly in advanced economies, and from some elements of potential financial contagion. In India, the adverse effects were mainly in the equity markets because of reversal of portfolio equity flows, and the concomitant effects on the domestic forex market and liquidity conditions. The macro effects were muted due to the overall strength of domestic demand, the healthy balance sheets of the Indian corporate sector, and the predominant domestic financing of investment.

In short, the combined impact of the reversal of portfolio equity flows, the reduced availability of international capital both debt and equity, the perceived increase in the price of equity with lower equity valuations, and pressure on the exchange rate, growth in the Indian corporate sector was impacted due to the global financial turmoil. On the other hand, on a macro basis, with external savings utilisation having been low traditionally, between 1 to 2 percent of GDP, and the sustained high domestic savings rate, this impact was at the margin. Moreover, the continued buoyancy of foreign direct investment suggested that confidence in Indian growth prospects remained healthy.

The process of de-leveraging and dysfunctional financial markets in the advanced economies accentuating a global financial crisis has highlighted the importance of orderly functioning of markets for achieving macroeconomic objectives. The equity markets followed the general global sentiments and market trends and after a phase of sharp downward movement, the market has shown recovery since then.

2.8 Achievements of Financial Sector Reforms

Financial sector in the Indian economy since the early 1990s has undergone a transformation towards a vibrant, competitive and diversified system, with a multiplicity of financial institutions having different risk profiles intermediating in various segments of the market spectrum. The evolution of the Indian financial system from somewhat of a constricted and an undersized one to a more open, deregulated and market oriented one and its interface with the growth process are the major areas of reforms still underway.

The financial system has exhibited considerable dynamism in recent years. The system today is varied, with a well-diversified structure of financial institutions, financial companies and mutual funds. The setting up of some specialised financial institutions and refinance institutions has provided depth to financial intermediation outside the banking sector. These developments, coupled with increased financial market liberalization, have enhanced competition. A number of existing financial institutions have diversified into several new activities, such as, investment banking and infrastructure financing, providing guarantees for domestic and offshore lending for infrastructure projects.

Rapid expansion of non-banking financial companies

(NBFCs) has taken place, providing avenues for depositors to hold assets and for borrowers to enhance the scale of funding of their activities. Various types of NBFCs have provided varied services that include equipment leasing, hire purchase, loans, investments, mutual benefit and chit fund activities. More recently, NBFCs activity has picked up in the area of housing finance.

Financial development is also reflected in the growing importance of mutual funds. In the 1990s, they enabled sizable mobilisation of financial surpluses of the households for investment in capital markets.

Capital markets themselves have become an important source of financing corporate investments, especially after firms were permitted to charge share premium in a flexible manner.

An understanding of the organisational structure of markets for financial assets is vital for knowing the limitations and prospects with regards to efficiency, integration and stability. Financial markets in India comprise, in the main: the credit market, the money market, the foreign exchange market, the debt market and the capital market. Recently, the derivatives market has also emerged. With banks having already been allowed to undertake insurance business, bancassurance market is also likely to emerge in a big way.

Most of the financial markets were characterised, till the early 1990s, by controls over the pricing of financial assets, restrictions on flows or transactions, barriers to entry, low liquidity and high transaction costs. These characteristics came in the way of development of the markets and allocative efficiency of resources channelled through them.

The initiation of financial sector reforms in the early 1990s was essentially to bring about a transformation in the structure, efficiency and stability of financial markets, as also an integration of the markets.

2.9 Areas of Concern

In spite of the significant improvements in the banking

industry as a result of reforms, several challenges lie ahead, the most important being the need to bring down the NPAs. Commercial banks continue to face the problem of non-performing assets (NPAs), attributable, *inter alia*, to factors such as weak debt recovery mechanism, non-realisation of collateral and poor credit appraisal techniques. Policy measures have not yielded the desired results. The enactment of the Securitisation and Reconstruction of Financial Assets and Enforcement of Security Interest Act, 2002 has increased the momentum for the recovery of NPAs. However, banks need to intensify their efforts to recover their overdues and prevent generation of fresh NPAs.

Co-operative banks constitute an important segment of the Indian banking system. They have an extensive branch network and reach out to people in remote areas. They have traditionally played an important role in creating banking habits among the lower and middle-income groups and in strengthening the rural credit delivery system. Unfortunately, financial reforms have not impacted the functioning of co-operative banks. Since the introduction of reforms, there has been very little perceptible improvement in either stability or efficiency of co-operative banks. In particular, the asset quality and profitability of co-operative banks has shown some deterioration in the reform period. Positive impact of reforms, as has been witnessed in the case of commercial banking sector, may take longer to get manifested for co-operative banks given the late start of the reform process in this sector.

Financial institutions, which constitute an important source of funds for the commercial sector, have been losing ground fast. The situation has come about as a result of the distinction between development and commercial banking getting blurred, high cost of funds and asset-liability mismatches. With reforms in the financial sector, the facility of low cost funds under long-term operations funds, funds from bilateral and multilateral agencies and bond issues under statutory liquidity ratio is no more available. Now the financial institutions are raising funds at market-related rates of interest. The Reserve Bank of India (RBI) has been advising financial institutions to chart a path for their evolution into universal banks. The merger of ICICI with the ICICI Bank was approved by the RBI in April 2002.

Competitive pressures as well as prudential regulatory requirements have made banks risk-averse, preferring their investment in relatively risk-free gilt instruments. The behaviour and strategies of bank business would need to change from the present so that they can factor in their own risk assessment even while performing their core activities. There is a need to ensure long term finance to support development and growth in the economy, even as restructuring takes place through mergers and universal banking.

To sum up, although the financial sector in India has grown fairly rapidly in recent years, in terms of the conventional metrics of financial deepening—such as a ratio of total financial claims or bank loans to GDP—India appears to be considerably behind other emerging markets. One of the most important gaps in our existing financial structure is the lack of a sufficiently large venture capital and angel investor community, which play an important role in financing start-ups, especially in areas where technology is the key to success and risk capital is needed.

Endnote

1. BS7799 is comprehensive in its coverage of security issues, containing a significant number of control requirements. Hence, compliance with it is a major task for most organisations. By following this standard, financial institutions including banks can ensure compliance to most of the information security requirements.

Part II
Banking Sector Evolution and Reforms

3

Reserve Bank of India

Central banks occupy a pivotal position in the institutional fabric of an economy. There is only one central bank in a country whose main function is to control the operations of the rest of the banking system. Reserve Bank of India (RBI), the central bank of India, is the apex institution responsible for managing and supervising the monetary and financial system of the economy.

3.1 Establishment and Early History of RBI

Imperial Bank of India, which emerged as a consequence of the amalgamation of three Presidency Banks of Bengal, Bombay and Madras in 1921, assumed certain central banking functions except currency management. The control of currency management continued to be with the Government of India in order to ensure that the central banking entity did not appropriate powers greater than those mandated by the political authority. The Reserve Bank of India Act was placed on the statute book on March 6, 1934. The RBI commenced operations on April 1, 1935 and was nationalised on January 1, 1949. The head office of the Bank is in Mumbai and its executive head is called the Governor.

The objective of establishing the RBI, as stated in the preamble to the RBI Act 1934, was to "regulate the issue of bank notes and the keeping of the reserves with a view to securing monetary stability in India and generally to operate the currency and credit system of the country to its advantage". The Bank's functions as laid down in the statutes were: (a) issue of currency (b) banker to Government; and (c) banker to other banks. Except in the sphere of agriculture, the Bank was not entrusted with any great promotional role and that too on a limited scale.

Central banks occupy a pivotal position in the institutional fabric of an economy. The functions of a modern central bank are vastly different from what was expected from the early central banks founded in Europe in the 17th century. The evolution of central banking in the Indian context has its own specificity. RBI, while discharging its statutory responsibilities, has played a crucial role in the nation building process, particularly in the development of the financial sector. In fact, institution building constitutes a distinguishing feature of central banking in India.

3.2 Functions of RBI

RBI performs all the major functions of a central bank and these are discussed below.

3.2.1 Sole Currency Authority: The management of currency is one of the core functions of a central bank and one, which commands a high degree of public visibility. This is especially so in a country like India, where people have a marked preference for cash transactions. The fact that there are a number of inaccessible pockets in the country adds to the already formidable challenges in managing currency in India.

In terms of the RBI Act, the affairs of the RBI relating to note issue and general banking business are conducted separately through Issue Department and Banking Department. The Issue Department is responsible for the aggregate value of the currency notes of the RBI in circulation from time to time and maintains the eligible assets for equivalent value. The mechanism of putting currency into circulation and its withdrawal from circulation (expansion and contraction of currency) is undertaken through the Banking Department.

Barring one-rupee notes and coins, RBI is the sole authority for the issue of currency in India. One rupee notes and coins are issued by the Central Government. However, their distribution to the public is the sole responsibility of the RBI. For the issue of notes, the RBI has a separate department, the Department of Issue. All the currency issued by the RBI is its monetary liability and is backed by assets of equal value.

Currency management by the RBI is currently passing through a modernisation phase. A number of significant steps have been taken in this sphere which includes the following.

1. Building up of the capacity of note printing presses.
2. Reforms in the operations of the Issue Department including in the note distribution network.
3. Introduction of new security features.
4. Shift towards higher denomination notes in circulation.

3.2.2 Banker to the Governments: Before the formation of the RBI, the Imperial Bank of India performed many of the functions as banker to the Government. With the establishment of the RBI, the Imperial Bank ceased to be the banker to the Government, but entered into an agreement with the RBI for providing its services as the sole agent of the RBI in places where it had a branch and there was no branch of the Banking Department of the RBI.

As the banker to the Central Government and to the State Governments by virtue of agreements entered into with them, the RBI provides a range of banking services for these Governments such as acceptance of money on government account payment/withdrawals of funds and collection and transfer of funds through different means. Sections 20, 21 and 21A of the RBI Act provide the statutory basis for these functions. The terms and conditions on which the RBI acts as banker to the Central and State Governments are set out in separate agreements, which the RBI entered into with these Governments.

RBI is the banker for all Governments in India (except Jammu and Kashmir). The RBI provides all those banking services to the Central and State Governments which a commercial bank ordinarily offers to its customers. The Governments keep their cash balances on current account deposit with the RBI and the latter carries out banking business involving receipts and payments of money on behalf of the Governments. The Governments are required, under agreement, to maintain a minimum balance with the RBI. It is the duty of the Finance Department of each Government to ensure that there are always sufficient funds in its bank account and that at no stage the cash balance falls short of the prescribed minimum.

3.2.3 Bankers' Bank and Lender-of-the-last-resort: Under the Reserve Bank of India Act, 1934 and the Banking Regulation Act, 1949, the RBI is vested with extensive powers of supervision, regulation, and control over commercial and co-operative banks. The regulatory functions of the RBI pertain to licensing, branch expansion, and amalgamation of commercial banks. The RBI calls for returns and other information from the commercial banks and periodically inspects their working.

The scheduled banks in India are required under law to deposit with the RBI a stipulated ratio (lying between 3 percent and 15 percent) of their total liabilities. These are compulsory reserves of banks with the RBI and are not available to them for meeting inter-bank clearing claims. The underlying philosophy of this statutory reserve requirement is that by varying it within limits, the RBI can use it as a weapon of monetary-credit control.

Reserves of the banks with the RBI may be used to meet the temporary cash needs of the commercial banks. Commercial banks are supposed to meet their shortfalls of cash from sources other than the RBI but in acute emergency they can approach the RBI for help and that is why the central bank is also called the lender-of-the-last-resort.

3.2.4 Controller of Money and Credit: Like other central banks, the core function of the RBI is to formulate and administer monetary policy to maintain the stability of the rupee. During Pre-Independence period, there was, however, no formal monetary policy formulation other than that of administering the supply and demand for credit in the economy. The Bank Rate [1], reserve requirements and open market operations [2] were the mechanisms for regulating the credit availability. The Bank Rate, as an instrument of control, was not used at all in this period, except once in November

1935 when the rate was reduced from 3.5 percent to 3.0 percent. The rate remained unchanged thereafter till November 1951. The RBI, however, employed the instruments of open market operations (OMOs) in a fairly substantial way. Although the RBI was vested with adequate powers to resort to the qualitative instruments, *viz.* selective credit control, no need was felt during the initial stages of its functioning due to the existence of price stability.

The RBI has multiple instruments at its command such as repo and reverse repo rates [3], cash reserve ratio (CRR), statutory liquidity ratio (SLR), open market operations, including the market stabilisation scheme (MSS) and the liquidity adjustment facility (LAF), special market operations, and sector-specific liquidity facilities. In addition, the RBI also uses prudential tools to modulate flow of credit to certain sectors consistent with financial stability. The availability of multiple instruments and flexible use of these instruments in the implementation of monetary policy has enabled the RBI to modulate the liquidity and interest rate conditions amidst uncertain global macroeconomic conditions.

An important function of RBI is to control money and credit in the country. The instruments of monetary control operated by the RBI may be classified into two categories: (a) quantitative or global or aggregative measures which affect the total amount of money supply and credit and (b) qualitative or selective measures which affect the allocation of bank credit among competing uses and users.

3.2.5 Controller of Foreign Exchange: The RBI is the custodian of the foreign exchange reserves of India. It manages exchange control and the external value of the rupee. The history of exchange control in India dates back to the outbreak of Second World War in 1939. The exchange control is operated in a manner so that the demand for foreign exchange is contained within the limits of its available supplies. In other words, the available foreign exchange is allocated among competing demands in such a way as to make its optimum use.

The need for this control and planned use arises in view of the general shortage of foreign exchange reserves in most developing countries. All foreign exchange transactions made by the RBI are at the official rates of exchange.

RBI has delegated considerable powers to the authorised dealers to release foreign exchange for a variety of purposes and has been focusing on the development of the foreign exchange market. In order to deepen the foreign exchange market, a large number of products have been introduced and the entry of newer players has been allowed. Additional hedging instruments, such as, foreign currency-rupee options have been introduced and authorised dealers have been permitted to use innovative products like cross-currency options, interest rate and currency swaps, caps/collars and forward rate agreements (FRAs) in the international forex market.

3.2.6 Source of Economic Information: RBI provides, through its publications, useful data and information on various aspects of the economy, particularly monetary and banking activities. Three important and regular publications of the RBI are: (a) Reserve Bank of India *Bulletin* (Monthly), (b) *Report on Currency and Finance* (Annual), and (c) *Handbook of Statistics on Indian Economy.*

3.2.7 Promotional Role of RBI: Apart from performing the customary functions of a central bank, the RBI has played an important role in building, consolidating, and strengthening the financial infrastructure of India. It has also played an effective role in influencing the allocation of credit in favour of priority sectors. Commercial banking facilities have been extended to small towns and rural areas as a result of the policies of the RBI.

RBI has paid special attention to the credit needs of the rural (agricultural) sector. Towards this end, the Agricultural Refinance and Development Corporation (ARDC) was set up as a wholly-owned subsidiary of the RBI in 1963. The National Bank for Agriculture and Rural Development (NABARD) is another example of the promotional role of the RBI in the agricultural sector. Similarly, the RBI promoted the cause of industrial finance by actively associating itself with such public sector undertakings as erstwhile Industrial Development Bank of India (IDBI). In the area of credit allocation, RBI has followed the policy of special consideration for priority sectors, like agriculture and small-scale industries, at concessional rates of interest and lenient collateral requirements.

3.3 Changing Role of RBI in the Financial Sector

Since the setting up of the Reserve Bank of India in 1935, its role in the financial sector and financial market development has undergone significant changes. Emerging primarily as a bank-based financial system, the development of financial structure in India has been to finance the planned development efforts. To this end, institutional development received considerable attention of the RBI. The broad-based development of the banking sector to meet short-term financing needs was supplemented by the setting up of specialised development finance institutions by the RBI to cater to long-term financing needs. Since the early 1990s, the introduction of financial sector reforms has provided a strong impetus to the development of financial markets. The introduction of market-based monetary policy instruments, the liberalisation of capital controls and integration of the Indian economy with global markets have exposed the country to potentially volatile capital inflows, posing new challenges and dilemmas for the RBI in monetary and exchange rate management.

RBI has been suitably reorienting the regulatory and supervisory framework so as to meet the challenges of a new environment. It has been the endeavour of the RBI to develop a competitive, strong and dynamic banking system so that it plays an effective role in supporting the growth process of the economy. The emphasis has been on safeguarding the financial stability of the overall system through increased emphasis on prudential guidelines and effective monitoring, improving institutional soundness, strengthening the regulatory and supervisory processes by aligning with international best practices and by developing the necessary technological and legal infrastructure. While the approach towards the reforms has essentially been gradual and relevant to the context, consultative processes and appropriate timing and sequencing of measures have succeeded in aiding growth, enhancing efficiency, avoiding crises and imparting resilience to the financial system.

The role of the RBI in the financial markets assumed significance due to the following factors.

1. The primary interest of the RBI in financial markets is because of its criticality in the transmission of monetary policy. From an operational perspective, reliance on indirect instruments and money market operations for conducting monetary policy necessitated development of the money, Government securities and foreign exchange markets.
2. Financial stability has emerged as one of the increasingly important concerns for the RBI resulting in increased attention to financial market development. The money market is the focal point for RBI intervention for equilibrating short-term liquidity flows on account of its linkages with the foreign exchange market. The Government securities market has become the focal point for the entire debt market due to several considerations: (a) the fiscal deficit of the Government, both Centre and the States, continues to be fairly high, resulting in large market borrowings by the Central and State Governments. With the corporate debt market still in its nascent stage of development, the Government securities market is the largest component of the debt market; (b) it serves as a benchmark for pricing of other debt market instruments and (c) it provides an efficient transmission channel for monetary policy.
3. Since the markets were repressed in several ways in the

past by law, regulation and policies, the RBI has, therefore, been facilitating the development of markets by creating an enabling environment through legal changes, technological and institutional development and dynamic improvements in market micro-structure.

4. Technological infrastructure has become an indispensable part of the reform of the financial markets, with the gradual development of sophisticated instruments and innovations in market practices. The RBI has, therefore, taken active interest in developing appropriate technological infrastructure to facilitate market development in areas such as payment and settlement systems, delivery *versus* payment (D*v*P) and electronic funds transfer (EFT).
5. Modern financial markets are complex. The RBI, therefore, needs to equip and continuously update itself to perform its developmental and regulatory roles effectively. The process involves constant interaction with the global counterparts in order to identify best practices, benchmark existing practices in the Indian markets, identify gaps and take measures to move towards international standards, within the framework of India's unique country circumstances.

3.4 Financial Sector Technology Vision Document

The RBI released the draft Financial Sector Technology Vision document on May 6, 2005. It provided a broad overview of the thrust areas of the direction provided by the RBI in respect of IT for the financial sector for more than two decades and sets out a roadmap for 2005-08. The Vision document focused on the following:

- IT for regulation and supervision.
- IT for the financial sector.
- IT for Government-related functions.

The Vision Document envisaged emerging challenges in the form of implementation of standardisation across a variety of hybrid systems at different financial entities, need for decision support systems and the technology to facilitate risk based off-site supervision. It envisioned common inter-operable web-based structures for transmission of data relating to regulatory functions and the use of a single centralised database for all information, apart from hiving off the operation of non-critical functions by the RBI.

The Vision Document also visualised Institute for Development and Research in Banking Technology (IDRBT) which is to be a premier research institute, concentrating on research and development for the banking and financial sector, providing educational/training facilities and hiving off business related activities.

Recognising the requirements of IT for the financial sector, the Vision Document elucidated thrust areas of the RBI by providing generic information on various standards and approaches, IS Audit and requisite focus on business continuity plans. The Vision Document proposed that specific attention would be devoted to percolation of technology efforts to all types of banks and all sections of the customers in the banks with specific reference to the rural areas and the use of affordable technology products which can be easily used by the target clientele with inter-shareable resources.

The document also detailed the use of IT in the Government sector transactions (which has the largest potential to grow significantly in the years to come), with specific attention on the need for business process re-engineering, changes in rules and procedures for aligning them with e-governance in a manner so as to achieve implementable objectives.

Endnotes

1. Bank Rate is defined as the standard rate at which the RBI is prepared to buy or discount the bills of exchange or other commercial paper eligible for purchase under Section 49 of the RBI Act.
2. Open Market Operations refer to buying and selling of securities by the RBI, particularly from/to the scheduled commercial banks, as part of the policy to maintain orderly coordination in the securities market.

3. Repo rate is the rate at which RBI repurchases government securities from banks. In return, banks get cash to meet their short-term requirements. When RBI wants to inject liquidity in the system it reduces the repo rate which also acts as the benchmark short-term lending rate.

4

Commercial Banks: Phases of Evolution and Reforms

Commercial banking in India during the pre-Independence period was largely characterised by the existence of private banks organised as joint stock companies. Most banks were small and had private shareholding of the closely-held variety. They were largely localised and many of them failed. They came under the purview of the RBI that was established as a central bank for the country in 1935. But the process of regulation and supervision was limited by the provisions of the RBI Act, 1934 and the Companies Act, 1913. The indigenous bankers and moneylenders had remained mainly isolated from the institutional part of the system. The usurious network was still rampant and exploitative. Co-operative credit was the only hope for credit in rural areas but the movement was successful only in a few regions.

4.1 Phase I: Early Years of Independence (1947-69)

As in several other developing countries, the financial system in India has traditionally been dominated by financial intermediaries, especially banking institutions. Banking in India has a long history and it has evolved over the years passing through various phases. At the time of Independence, the Indian banking system was weak. The entire banking sector was in the private sector and the credit requirements of agriculture and other needy sectors were ignored.

The period soon after Independence posed several challenges to the Indian economy including the virtual absence of institutional credit facilities in the vast rural areas of the country. Further, the non-availability of adequate assets made it difficult for people to approach banks. In 1951, India launched its First Five Year Plan (1951-56) which accorded high priority to the development of rural India, particularly agriculture. The All India Rural Credit Survey Committee recommended the creation of a State-partnered and State-sponsored bank by taking over the Imperial Bank of India and integrating with it the former State-owned or State-associated banks. Accordingly, an Act was passed in the Parliament in May 1955 and the State Bank of India was constituted on July 1, 1955. Later, the State Bank of India (Subsidiary Banks) Act was passed in 1959 enabling the State Bank of India to take over eight former State-associated banks as its subsidiaries.

During this period, the industrial sector claimed the lion's share in bank credit. Within the industry, the large-scale sector cornered the bulk of credit and the share of small-scale industries was marginal. There were many reasons for the dominance of large industrial companies in the banking sector. Firstly, many commercial banks were under the ownership/control of big industrial houses.

Secondly, through common directors (called interlocking of directorship), many commercial banks were connected with industrial and business houses, facilitating the flow of credit to large industries. Thirdly, the established industrial houses could obtain industrial licenses easily and on that basis, appropriate long-term bank credit.

A disturbing feature of the banking policy during this period was the negligible share of agricultural sector in bank credit. This share hovered around 2 percent of total commercial bank credit. The privately-owned commercial banks were neither interested nor geared to meet the risky and small credit requirements of the farmers. Similarly, the share of other non-industrial sectors in bank credit was also low. Since the commercial banks were under the control of big industrialists, the lendable funds of the banks were sometimes used to finance socially undesirable activities like hoarding of essential commodities.

4.2 Phase II: From Nationalisation of Banks Till Initiation of Banking Sector Reforms (1969-91)

With a view to better aligning the banking system to the needs of planning and economic policy, the policy of social control over the banking sector began in 1967. The year 1969 was a landmark in the history of commercial banking in India. In July of that year, the government nationalised 14 major commercial banks of the country. In April 1980, government nationalised 6 more commercial banks. Leading commercial banks of the country were nationalised with the following objectives in view.

1. To break the ownership and control of banks by a few business families.
2. To prevent concentration of wealth and economic power.
3. To mobilise savings of the masses from every nook and corner of the country.
4. To pay greater attention to the credit needs of the priority sectors like agriculture and small industries.

With the nationalisation of these banks, the major segment of the banking sector came under the control of the Government. Massive expansion of the branch network that followed the nationalisation of banks resulted in large deposit mobilisation by banks, which helped in stepping up the overall savings rate of the economy. However, during this period, a major portion of resources of the banks were pre-empted at below market rates by way of directed credit and directed investments. Profitability of the banking sector was, therefore, affected. Banks were also saddled with large non-performing assets. Their capital base also became weak.

The nationalisation of banks was an attempt to use the scarce resources of the banking system for the purpose of planned development. The task of maintaining a large number of small accounts was not profitable for the banks as a result of which they had limited lending in the rural sector. The problem of lopsided distribution of banks and the lack of explicit articulation of the need to channel credit to certain priority sectors was sought to be achieved through nationalisation policy. The Lead Bank Scheme provided the blueprint of further bank branch expansion.

The course of evolution of the banking sector in India since 1969 has been dominated by the nationalisation of banks. This period was characterised by rapid branch expansion that helped to draw the channels of monetary transmission far and wide across the country. The share of unorganised credit fell sharply and the economy seemed to come out of low level equilibrium trap. However, the stipulations that made this possible and helped spread institutional credit and nurture the financial system, also led to distortions in the process. The administered interest rates and the burden of directed lending constrained the banking sector significantly. There was very little operational flexibility for the commercial banks. Profitability occupied a back seat. Banks also suffered from poor governance. Fortunately, for the Indian economy, quick action was taken to address these issues.

The biggest achievement of nationalisation was the reallocation of sectoral credit in favour of agriculture, small industries and exports which formed the core of the priority sector. Within agriculture, credit for the procurement of food grains (food credit) was a major item. Other agricultural activities preferred for credit included poultry farming, dairy, and piggeries. Certain other sectors of the economy which also received attention for credit allocation were: professionals and self-employed persons, artisans and weaker sections of society. Conversely, there was a sharp fall in bank credit to large-scale industries. However, the share of small-scale industry registered an upward trend.

Nationalisation of commercial banks was a mixed blessing. After nationalisation there was a shift of emphasis from industry to agriculture. The country witnessed rapid expansion in bank branches, even in rural areas. Branch expansion programme led to mobilisation of savings from all parts of the country. Nationalised banks were able to pay attention to the credit needs of weaker sections, artisans and self-employed. However, bank nationalisation created its own problems like excessive bureaucratisation, red-tapism and disruptive tactics of trade unions of bank employees.

4.3 Phase III: Banking Sector Reforms since 1991

The period beginning from the early 1990s witnessed the transformation of the banking sector as a result of financial sector reforms that were introduced as a part of structural reforms initiated in 1991. The reform process in the financial sector was undertaken with the prime objective of having a strong and resilient banking system. The progress achieved in the areas of strengthening the regulatory and supervisory norms has ushered in greater accountability and market discipline amongst the participants.

The RBI has made sustained efforts towards adoption of international benchmarks in a gradual manner, as appropriate to the Indian conditions, in various areas such as prudential norms, risk management, supervision, corporate governance and transparency and disclosures. The reform process has helped in taking the management of the banking sector to the level, where the RBI ceased to micro-manage commercial banks and focused largely on the macro goals. The focus on deregulation and liberalisation coupled with enhanced responsibilities for banks made the banking sector resilient and capable of facing several newer global challenges.

4.4 Backdrop of Banking Sector Reforms

Until the early 1990s, the banking sector suffered from lack of competition, low capital base, low productivity and high intermediation cost. Prior to reforms, the Indian Government determined the quantum, allocation and the price of credit, a situation referred to as *financial repression* by some experts.

It was in this backdrop, that wide-ranging banking sector reforms in India were introduced as an integral part of the economic reforms initiated in the early 1990s. Reforms in the commercial banking sector had two distinct phases.

The first phase of reforms—implemented subsequent to the

release of the Report of the Committee on Financial System (Chairman: M. Narasimham), 1992 (or Narasimham Committee I)—focussed mainly on enabling and strengthening measures. The Committee was guided by the fundamental assumption that the resources of the banks come from the general public and held by the banks in trust. These resources have to be deployed for maximum benefit of their owners, i.e. the depositors. This assumption automatically implies that even the Government has no business to endanger the solvency, health and efficiency of the nationalised banks.

According to the Committee, the poor financial shape and low efficiency of public sector banks was due to: (a) extensive degree of central direction of their operations, particularly in terms of investment, credit allocation and branch expansion, and (b) excessive political interference, resulting into failure of commercial banks to operate on the basis of their commercial judgement and in the framework of internal economy. Despite opposition from trade unions and some political parties, the Government accepted all the major recommendations of the Committee some of which have already been implemented.

The second phase of reforms—implemented subsequent to the recommendations of the Committee on Banking Sector Reforms (Chairman: M. Narasimham), 1998 (or Narasimham Committee II)—placed greater emphasis on structural measures and improvement in standards of disclosure and levels of transparency in order to align the Indian standards with international best practices.

4.5 Objectives of Banking Sector Reforms

The key objective of reforms in the banking sector in India has been to enhance the stability and efficiency of banks. To achieve this objective, various reform measures were initiated that could be categorised broadly into three main groups: (a) enabling measures, (b) strengthening measures, and (c) institutional measures.

Enabling measures were designed to create an environment

where banks could respond optimally to market signals on the basis of commercial considerations. Salient among these included reduction in statutory pre-emptions so as to release greater funds for commercial lending, interest rate deregulation to enable price discovery, granting of operational autonomy to banks and liberalisation of the entry norms for financial intermediaries.

Strengthening measures aimed at reducing the vulnerability of banks in the face of fluctuations in the economic environment. These included, *inter alia*, capital adequacy, income recognition, asset classification and provisioning norms, exposure norms, improved levels of transparency, and disclosure standards.

Institutional framework conducive to development of banks needs to be developed. Salient among these include reforms in the legal framework pertaining to banks and creation of new institutions.

4.6 Components of Banking Sector Reforms

With a view to overcoming several weaknesses that had crept into the system over the years and with a view to creating a strong, competitive and vibrant banking system, several measures, including the following, were initiated beginning the early 1990s. Banking sector reforms since 1991 have included, among others, the following.

1. Granting operational autonomy to banks.
2. Reduction in statutory pre-emptions so as to release greater funds for commercial lending.
3. Deregulation of interest rates.
4. Relaxation in investment norms for banks.
5. Easing of restrictions in respect of banks' foreign currency investments.
6. Withdrawal of reserve requirements on inter-bank borrowings.
7. Introduction of prudential norms in line with international best practices.
8. Allowing entry of new private sector banks and enhanced presence of foreign banks.

9. Allowing public sector banks to access the capital market and providing to them operational flexibility and functional autonomy.
10. Revamping of supervisory system for creating a sound banking system.
11. Strengthening corporate governance practices and disclosure standards of banks.

As a result of above measures, the size and structure of the banking sector has undergone a significant change. Financial repression has eased substantially with the deregulation of interest rates and substantial removal of credit allocation.

4.6.1 Deregulation of Deposit and Lending Interest Rates: Narasimham Committee-I had recommended that the level and structure of interest rates in the country should be broadly determined by market forces. All controls and regulations on interest rates should be removed.

The process of deregulation of domestic deposit rates began when banks were allowed to set interest rates for maturities between 15 days and up to 1 year subject to a ceiling of 8 percent effective April 1985. However, this freedom was withdrawn by end-May 1985 in the face of an ensuing price war. The process of deregulation was resumed in April 1992 by replacing the existing maturity-wise prescriptions by a single ceiling rate of 13 percent for all deposits above 46 days. The ceiling rate was brought down to 10 percent in November 1994, but was raised to 12 percent in April 1995. Banks were allowed to fix the interest rates on deposits with maturity of over 2 years in October 1995 which was further relaxed to maturity of over one year in July 1996.

In October 1997, the deposit rates were fully deregulated. Consequently, the RBI gave the freedom to commercial banks to fix their own interest rates on domestic term deposits of various maturities with the prior approval of their respective boards of directors/Asset Liability Management Committee. Banks were permitted to determine their own penal interest rates for premature withdrawal of domestic term deposits and the restrictions on banks that they must offer the same rate on deposits of the same maturity irrespective of the size of deposits was removed in respect of deposits of ₹ 15 lakh and above in April 1998 with the laying down of policy in this regard by the board of the bank. Presently, banks have complete freedom in fixing their domestic deposit rates, except interest rate on savings deposits which continues to be regulated and is currently fixed at 4 percent.

Prime lending rates of banks for commercial credit are now entirely within the purview of the banks and are not set by the RBI. The country has moved towards liberalised credit allocation mechanism and reduced direct control over interest rates by the monetary authorities. The purpose of deregulation is to promote healthy competition among the banks and encourage their operational efficiency.

4.6.2 Organisation of Banking Structure: Narasimham Committee I proposed a substantial reduction in the number of public sector banks through mergers and acquisitions. The broad pattern should consist of the following.

1. 3 or 4 large banks which could become international in character.
2. 8 or 10 national banks with a network of branches throughout the country.
3. Local banks whose operations would be generally confined to a specific region.
4. Rural banks whose operations will be confined to rural areas.

Significantly, Narasimham Committee I recommended that RBI should permit the setting up of new banks in the private sector. It wanted a positive declaration from the Government that there would be no more nationalisation of banks. It further recommended that there should not be any difference in treatment between the public sector banks and the private sector banks.

It recommended that RBI should follow a more liberal policy in respect of allowing the foreign banks to open branches in India and they should be subjected to the same requirements as are applicable to the Indian banks.

In January 1993, RBI had issued guidelines for licensing of new banks in the private sector. It had granted licenses to 10 banks which are presently in business. Based on a review of experience gained on the functioning of new private sector banks, revised guidelines were issued in January 2000. Following are the major revised provisions.

1. Initial minimum paid-up capital shall be ₹ 200 crore which will be raised to ₹ 300 crore within three years of commencement of business.
2. Contribution of promoters shall be a minimum of 40 percent of the paid-up capital of the bank at any point of time. This contribution of 40 percent shall be locked in for five years from the date of licensing of the bank.
3. While augmenting capital to ₹ 300 crore within three years, promoters shall bring in at least 40 percent of the fresh capital which will also be locked in for five years.
4. NRI participation in the primary equity of a new bank shall be to the maximum extent of 40 percent.

4.6.3 Duality of Control: Narasimham Committee I recommended removal of duality of control over the banking system by the banking department of the Finance Ministry on the one hand, and by the RBI on the other hand. The Committee desired the RBI to assume full responsibility of overseeing the functioning of the banking system.

4.6.4 Abolition of Selective Credit Controls (SCCs): SCCs, introduced in India in 1956, pertain to regulation of credit for specific purposes. The techniques of SCCs used by the RBI include fixing minimum margins for lending against securities, ceiling on maximum advances to individual borrowers against stocks of certain commodities, and minimum discriminatory rates of interest prescribed for certain kinds of advances. SCCs have been used mainly to prevent the speculative holding of essential commodities like foodgrains to prevent price rise.

Selective credit controls have been abolished in the post-liberalisation period.

4.6.5 Managerial Autonomy for Public Sector Banks: Competition among the commercial banks has increased with the entry of private sector banks, permission to foreign banks to open up to 12 branches a year with effect from 1998-99 and relaxation of various restrictions on public sector banks which, *inter alia,* are now allowed to access the capital market to raise funds. This will dilute the shareholding of the Government.

In the changed scenario, public sector banks will have to improve their efficiency. The highly regulated and directed banking system is now transforming itself into one characterised by openness, competition and prudence. This development conforms to the liberalisation and globalisation needs of the Indian economy.

The Government of India issued a managerial autonomy package for the public sector banks on February 22, 2005 with a view to providing them a level playing field with the private sector banks in India. Under the new framework, the Boards of public sector banks would enjoy more freedom to carry out their functions efficiently without any impediment. The functions, however, have to be in sync with the extant statutory requirements, government policy prescription and regulatory guidelines issued by the RBI from time to time. The revised guidelines allow the following to public sector banks.

1. Pursue new lines of business.
2. Make suitable acquisitions of companies or businesses.
3. Close/merge unviable branches.
4. Open overseas offices.
5. Set up subsidiaries.
6. Exit a line of business.

Similarly, these banks have been allowed to decide human resource issues, including staffing pattern, recruitment, placement, transfer, training, promotions and pensions as well as visits to foreign countries to interact with investors, depositors and other stakeholders. Besides, the boards of directors of stronger banks would have additional autonomy for framing their own human resource (HR) policies. Prescription of standards for categorisation of branches, based on volume of business and other relevant factors, have been left to the banks to decide. Public sector banks have been permitted to lay down policy of accountability and responsibility of bank officials.

Public sector banks (PSBs) continued to be a dominant part of the banking system. As on March 31, 2018, the PSBs accounted for 65.79 percent of the total liabilities/assets of the scheduled commercial banking system. A unique feature of the reform of the public sector banks was the process of their financial restructuring. The banks were recapitalised by the government to meet prudential norms through recapitalisation bonds. Divestment of equity and offer to private shareholders was undertaken through a public offer and not by sale to strategic investors.

Thus, all the PSBs which issued shares to private shareholders, have been listed on the exchanges and are subject to the same disclosure and market discipline standards as other listed entities. To address the problem of distressed assets, a mechanism has been developed to allow sale of these assets to asset reconstruction companies which operate as independent commercial entities.

It needs to be noted that the turnaround in the financial performance of the public sector banks, pursuant to the banking sector reforms, has resulted in the market valuation of government holdings in these banks far exceeding the initial recapitalisation cost—which is something unique to the Indian banking system. Thus, the recapitalisation of banks by the government has not been merely a *holding out* operation by the majority owner of the banks. The Indian experience has shown that a strong, pragmatic and non-discriminatory regulatory framework coupled with the market discipline effected through the listing of the equity shares and operational autonomy provided to the banks, can have a significant positive impact on the functioning of the public sector banks.

4.6.6 Other Measures: Credit restrictions for purchase of consumer durables have been removed/relaxed. Similarly, coverage of priority sector has been enlarged by the inclusion of software, agro-processing industries and venture capital. These measures have given the banks the much-needed flexibility to manage their asset portfolios.

In response to reforms, the Indian banking sector has undergone radical transformation during the 1990s. Reforms have altered the organizational structure, ownership pattern and domain of operations of institutions and infused competition in the financial sector. The competition has forced the institutions to reposition themselves in order to survive and grow. The extensive progress in technology has enabled markets to graduate from outdated systems to modern market design, thus, bringing about a significant reduction in the speed of execution of trades and transaction costs.

In terms of the average capital adequacy ratio for the scheduled commercial banks, which was around 2 percent in 1997, had increased to 11.7 percent as on March 31, 2018. The improvement in the capital adequacy ratio has come about despite significant growth in the aggregate assets of the banking system. This level of capital ratio in the Indian banking system compares quite well with the banking system in many other countries.

In regard to the asset quality also, the gross NPAs of the scheduled commercial banks, which were as high as 15.7 percent at end-March 1997, have declined to 11.2 percent as at end-March 2018. The net NPAs of these banks during the same period declined from 8.1 percent to 6.0 percent. These figures too compare favourably with the international trends and have been driven by the improvements in loan loss provisioning by the banks, certain institutional measures, as also by the improved recovery climate enabled by the legislative environment.

The reform measures have also resulted in an improvement in the profitability of banks. The return on assets (RoA) of scheduled commercial banks has remained stagnant from 0.4 percent in the year 1991-92 to 0.4 percent in 2016-17. The Indian banks would appear well placed in this regard too vis-à-vis the broad range of RoA for the international banks.

The banking sector reforms also emphasised the need to improve productivity of the banks through appropriate rationalisation measures so as to reduce the operating cost and improve the profitability. A variety of initiatives were taken by the banks, including adoption of modern technology, which has resulted in improved productivity. The business per employee (BPE), as a measure of productivity, for the public sector banks has registered considerable improvement.

The Indian experience has shown that a strong, pragmatic and non-discriminatory regulatory framework coupled with the market discipline effected through the listing of the equity shares and operational autonomy provided to the banks, can have a significant positive impact on the functioning of the public sector banks.

5

Commercial Banks: Credit Allocation Policies, Supervision and Migration to Basel Norms

5.1 Credit Allocation Policies

Credit market, with commercial banks as its predominant segment, has been the major source for meeting the finance requirements in the economy, both for the private sector and the public sector enterprises. The year 1969 was a landmark in the history of commercial banking in India. In July of that year, the Government nationalised 14 major commercial banks of the country. In April 1980, Government nationalised 6 more banks. The credit policy underwent drastic changes after that historic event. For a few decades preceding the onset of banking and financial sector reforms in early 1990s, credit institutions operated in an environment that was heavily regulated and characterised by barriers to entry, which protected them against competition.

The issue of allocation of bank resources among various sectors was addressed through mechanisms such as statutory liquidity ratio (SLR), Credit Authorisation Scheme (CAS), fixation of maximum permissible bank finance (MPBF) and selective credit controls. This regulated environment set in complacency in the manner in which credit institutions operated and responded to the customer needs. The interest rate played a very limited role as the equilibrating mechanism between demand and supply of resources. The resource allocation process was deficient, which manifested itself in poor asset quality. Credit institutions also lacked operational flexibility and functional autonomy.

5.1.1 Allocation of Credit between Government and the Private Sector: Commercial banks provide credit to the government in two ways. Firstly, they provide funds to the Central and the State Governments through investment in government bonds. The commercial banks (along with LIC, GIC, etc.) are part of the 'captive market' for government securities because they are statutorily required to invest a certain minimum proportion of their total assets in government securities. Commercial banks are subject not only to cash reserve requirements, but are also subject to statutory liquidity ratio.

Secondly, commercial banks also make loans and advances to public sector units. They also invest in market bonds issued by public sector enterprises. As a result of the increasing claim of government and public sector units on commercial bank credit, the share of private sector in bank credit has declined. The private sector has to rely more and more on equity and debenture capital to meet their needs.

5.1.2 Inter-sectoral Allocation of Institutional Credit: Sectoral classification refers to main sectors of the economy in terms of economic activity. These sectors are: (a) industry, (b) agriculture, (c) trade, and (d) miscellaneous services. Each such sector may be sub-divided into sub-sectors as, for example, industry into large scale industry and small-scale industry. In addition to sharing of resources between the private and the public sectors, a significant proportion of credit by commercial banks is earmarked for the priority sector. Priority sector comprises agriculture (both direct and indirect), small scale industries, small roads and water transport operators, small business, retail trade, professional and self-employed persons, state sponsored organisations for scheduled castes/scheduled tribes, education, housing (both direct and indirect), consumption loans, micro-credit, loans to software, and food and agro-processing sector.

5.1.3 Inter-regional Allocation of Credit: As regards inter-regional (i.e. State-wise) allocation of credit, there is a long-standing complaint of the poorer states that their share in total credit is meagre. Since most industrial and commercial activities are concentrated in developed states like Maharashtra, Gujarat and Karnataka therefore the flow of bank credit to these states is more, at least in terms of per capita credit allocation. In this context, it can be observed that credit policy has not been very successful in promoting regional balanced development of the country. With the new banking policy of the Government permitting private sector and foreign sector banks, the situation may worsen so far as backward states are concerned.

5.1.4 Priority Sector Lending: Directed lending through efforts such as the priority sector lending (PSL) programme of the Reserve Bank of India (RBI) have had a well-established history across many countries at different points in their development and have served a different purpose in each country. In India, while priority sector focus has existed from the 1950s in some form or the other, the PSL programme in its current form was implemented by the RBI in 1974, when banks were advised to raise credit to specified priority sectors of the economy to the level of 33.3 percent by March 1979. This number stands at 40 percent with the sectoral allocation specified in Table 5.1.

5.2 Regulation/Supervision since 1991

The decade of the 1990s was a watershed in the history of the Indian financial system in general and the banking system in particular. Notwithstanding the remarkable progress made by the Indian banking system in achieving social goals during the 1980s, it experienced certain problems that led to decline in efficiency and productivity, and erosion of profitability. Factors such as directed investment and directed credit programmes affected the operational efficiency of the banking system. The quality of loan portfolio also deteriorated.

The functional efficiency was affected due to over-staffing, inadequate progress in inducting technology and weaknesses in internal organisational structure of the banks. These factors necessitated urgent reforms in the financial system. Accordingly, a Committee on the Financial System (Chairman: M. Narasimham) was constituted in 1991 to look into various issues related to banking with a view to initiating wide ranging financial sector reforms. Following the Report of the Narasimham Committee, the RBI adopted a comprehensive approach on the reforms of the financial sector.

Table 5.1: Priority Sector Allocation of Credit

Sector	Percent of Adjusted Net Bank Credit (ANBC)	Remarks
Direct agriculture	13.5 percent	
Indirect agriculture	4.5 percent to qualify within agriculture and excess as part of the overall 40 percent target	
Small and medium enterprises (SMEs)	Within the overall 40 percent target	Sub-targets based on the size of the SMEs
Weaker sections	10 percent	Up to ₹ 50,000 for segments such as distressed farmers, scheduled castes (SCs), scheduled tribes (STs), and women

Source: Report of the Committee on Comprehensive Financial Services for Small Businesses and Low Income Households, (Chairman: Nachiket Mor), January 2014, Table 4.8.1, p. 118.

The Department of Supervision (DoS)—now called Department of Banking Supervision (DBS)—was set up within the RBI in 1993 to strengthen the institutional framework. A high powered Board for Financial Supervision (BFS), comprising the Governor of RBI as Chairman, one of the Deputy Governors as Vice-Chairman and four Directors of the Central Board of the

RBI as members was constituted in November 1994.

Measures such as deregulation of interest rates, reduction of statutory pre-emptions such as CRR and SLR, and provision of operational autonomy to the banks were taken to strengthen the banks. Further, various prudential measures that conformed to the global best practices were also implemented. One of the major objectives of banking sector reforms has been to enhance efficiency and productivity through enhanced competition. Guidelines to facilitate entry of the private sector banks were issued in 1993 to foster greater competition with a view to achieve higher productivity and efficiency of the banking system.

5.3 Migration to Basel Norms

5.3.1 Introduction: Internationally, there were no explicit capital adequacy standards before the introduction of Basel I norms in 1988. The most common approach was to lay down minimum capital requirements for banks in the respective banking legislations and determine the relative strength of capital position of a bank by ratios such as debt-equity ratio, or its other variants for measuring the level of leverage.

In the autumn of 1974, the Bank of England began to conceptualise the formation of a G-10 group of bank supervisors leading to the formation of the Standing Committee on Banking Regulation and Supervisory Practices, or the Basel Committee, in December 1974. The initial mandate of the Committee was for sharing of and application of each others knowledge, rather than any comprehensive attempt to harmonise cross-country supervision. Nevertheless, it led to an unimaginable degree of regulatory harmonisation later.

5.3.2 Basel I Norms: In December 1987 International Convergence of Capital Measures and Capital Standards, i.e. Basel Accord (now Basel I) was achieved. In July 1988, the Basel I Capital Accord was created.

The major achievement of the Basel Capital Accord 1988 was the introduction of discipline through imposition of risk-based capital standards both as measure of the strength of banks and as a trigger device for intervention by supervisors under the scheme of prompt corrective action (PCA).

Over the years, however, several deficiencies of the design of the Basel I framework surfaced. The Basel I capital adequacy norms were criticised for the simple *one-size-fits-all* approach that did not adequately differentiate between assets that have different risk levels. Despite the amendment to the original framework in 1996, the simple risk weighting approach of Basel I did not keep pace with more advanced risk measurement approaches at large banking organisations. By the late 1990s, some large banking organisations, especially in advanced countries, had begun developing economic capital models, which used quantitative methods to estimate the amount of capital required to support various elements of risks of an organization.

The Basel Committee itself recognised the deficiencies in the Basel I framework. The rapid rate of innovation in financial markets and the growing complexity of financial transactions reduced the relevance of Basel I as a risk managing framework, especially for large and complex banking organisations. Various shortcomings also distorted the behaviour of banks and made it much more complicated to monitor them.

Given the financial innovations and growing complexity of financial transactions and also with a view to addressing the shortcomings of Basel I, the Basel Committee on Banking Supervision (BCBS) released the New Capital Adequacy Framework for International Convergence of Capital Measurement and Capital Standards (Basel II) on June 26, 2004 to replace the 1988 Capital Accord by year-end 2007. Basel II norms aim at aligning minimum capital requirements to underlying risk profiles of banks. The framework was also designed to create incentives for better risk measurement and management.

5.3.3 Basel II Norms: While the Basel I framework was confined to the minimum capital requirements for banks, the

Basel II accord expands this approach to include two additional areas, *viz.* the supervisory review process and increased disclosure requirements for banks. In terms of Basel II, the stability of the banking system rests on the following three pillars, which are designed to reinforce each other:

Pillar 1: Minimum Capital Requirements—a largely new, risk-adequate calculation of capital requirements which (for the first time) explicitly includes operational risk in addition to market and credit risk.

Pillar 2: Supervisory Review Process (SRP)—the establishment of suitable risk management systems in banks and their review by the supervisory authority.

Pillar 3: Market Discipline—increased transparency due to expanded disclosure requirements for banks.

The central focus of this framework as in Basel I, continues to be credit risk. In the revised framework, the minimum regulatory capital requirements take into account not just credit risk and market risk, but also operational risk. The measures for credit risk are more complex, for market risk they are the same, while those for operational risk are new. Besides, Basel II includes certain Pillar 2 risks such as credit concentration risks and liquidity risks.

Apart from an increase in the number of risks, banks are required to achieve a more comprehensive risk management framework. While Basel I required lenders to calculate a minimum level of capital based on a single risk weight for each of the limited number of asset classes, the capital requirements are more risk sensitive under Basel II. The credit risk weights are related directly to the credit rating of each counterparty instead of the counterparty category.

Basel II capital adequacy rules are based on a *menu* approach that allows differences in approaches in relationship to the nature of banks and the nature of markets in which they operate. The minimum requirements for the advanced approaches are technically more demanding and require extensive databases and more sophisticated risk management techniques. Basel II prescriptions have ushered in a transition from capital adequacy to capital efficiency which implies that banks adopt a more dynamic use of capital, in which capital will flow quickly to its most efficient uses. Unlike Basel I, Basel II was quite complex as it offered choices, some of which involved application of quantitative techniques.

The revised framework is designed to provide options to banks and banking systems for determining the capital requirements for credit risk, market risk and operational risk. It enables banks/supervisors to select approaches that are most appropriate for their operations and financial markets. The revised framework is expected to promote adoption of stronger risk management practices in banks. Under Basel II, capital requirements of banks will be more closely aligned with the underlying risks in the balance sheets of banks. One of the important features of the revised framework is the emphasis on operational risk.

Operational risk is defined as the risk of loss resulting from inadequate or failed internal processes, people and systems or from external events. This definition includes legal risk, but excludes strategic and reputational risks. Operational risk differs from other banking risks in that it is typically not directly taken in return for an expected reward but is implicit in the ordinary course of corporate activity and has the potential to affect the risk management process. The Basel Committee identified the following seven types of operational risk events that have the potential to result in substantial losses.

1. Internal fraud.
2. External fraud.
3. Employment practices and workplace safety.
4. Clients, products and business practices.
5. Damage to physical assets.
6. Business disruption and system failures.
7. Execution, delivery and process management.

The potential losses, in turn, vary according to the business line within the bank in which the event occurs.

Management of specific operational risks is not new. It has always been important for banks to try to prevent fraud, maintain the integrity of internal controls, reduce errors in transaction processing and so on. However, what is relatively new is the thrust on operational risk management as a comprehensive practice comparable to the management of credit risk and market risk. To manage operational risk, banks are gradually gearing to develop risk assessment techniques that are appropriate to the size and complexities of portfolios, their resources and data availability.

5.3.4 Implementation of Basel Norms in India: India has been adopting international best practices in the area of regulation and supervision with a view to strengthening the banking sector. Following the Basel Accord of 1988, the capital to risk-weighted assets ratio (CRAR)—which took into account the element of risk involved in both balance sheet as well as off-balance sheet business—emerged as a well-recognised and universally accepted measure of soundness of the banking system. Accordingly, as a part of banking sector reforms, India adopted the Basel norms in a phased manner. In fact, India went a step further and stipulated CRAR at 9 percent as against the international norm of 8 percent. Furthermore, India also prescribed the capital charge for market risk in June 2004, broadly in line with the 1996 amendment to Basel norms.

In order to ensuring migration to Basel II in a non-disruptive manner, given the complexities involved, a consultative approach was followed. The RBI released draft guidelines for implementation of Basel II in India on February 15, 2005. In terms of the draft guidelines, banks were required to adopt standardised approach for credit risk and basic indicator approach for operational risk. The standardised duration method would continue to be applied to arrive at the capital charge for market risk. Banks would need the RBI's approval for migration to advanced approaches of risk measurement.

With a view to ensuring smooth transition to the revised

framework and providing opportunity to banks to streamline their systems and strategies, banks were required to commence a parallel run of the revised framework with effect from April 1, 2006. All scheduled commercial banks (except regional rural banks) were required to implement the revised capital adequacy framework with effect from March 31, 2007. However, Basel II framework in India became fully operational from end-March 2009.

Several measures were undertaken by the RBI to prepare the banking system to make a smooth migration to Basel II. Following the amendment to the Banking Companies (Acquisition and Transfer of Undertakings) Act in 1994, several public sector banks (PSBs) have raised capital both in India and abroad through global depository receipts (GDRs). Several PSBs have also raised subordinated debt through the private placement. Concurrently, a series of regulatory initiatives were taken by the RBI relevant for Basel II.

First, concerted efforts were made to ensure that the banks had suitable risk management framework oriented towards their requirements, dictated by the size and complexity of business, risk philosophy, market perceptions and the expected level of capital. Second, risk based supervision (RBS) was introduced in 23 banks on a pilot basis. Third, the RBI encouraged the banks to formalise their Internal Capital Adequacy Assessment Programme (ICAAP) in alignment with their business plans and performance budgeting system. Fourth, there has been a marked improvement in the area of disclosures, so as to have greater transparency in the financial position and risk profile of banks. Similarly, capacity building for ensuring the regulator's ability for identifying and permitting eligible banks to adopt internal ratings based/advanced measurement approaches was given due priority.

5.3.5 Migration to Advanced Approaches: Challenges: Having regard to the state of preparedness of the system, India has adopted only the simpler approaches available under the Framework. The RBI is yet to announce the timeframe for adoption of the Advanced Approaches in the Indian banking system but the migration to these Approaches is the eventual goal for which the banking system will need to start its preparations in all earnestness.

The migration to Advanced Approaches poses several significant challenges to the bankers and also to the RBI, being the banking regulator and supervisor.

First challenge is the availability of long time-series data for computing the risk parameters required under the Advanced Approaches. Good-quality, consistent and reliable data and information relating to the loan portfolios of the banks, as also sophisticated IT resources, are critical to the proper risk assessment under the Basel II framework. Data limitation is a key impediment to the design and implementation of credit risk models. This may prove to be a major challenge for the RBI and the banking sector, given the wide-spread branch network, though the increasing computerisation in the banking industry should prove to be of great help.

Second challenge is that the Advanced Approaches for credit risk and operational risk envisaged under the Basel II Framework require use of risk models by the banks. This, in turn, requires internal validation of these models by the banks themselves as also by the supervisors before the models can be permitted to be used for regulatory capital purposes. Such a validation process demands expert skills which need to be developed and nurtured.

Third challenge is that since Basel II Framework is primarily about ensuring robust risk management in the banks, its effective implementation, particularly the Advanced Approaches, will demand rapid and significant upgradation of skills, both at the level of the banking system as also within the RBI. In this context, banks are likely to face multi-faceted challenges, viz. assessing skill requirements, identifying and bridging the gaps, identifying talents, putting the available talents to optimum use, attracting fresh talents, and retention of talents. Banks would, therefore, need to pay special attention to strengthening their risk management infrastructure in all its dimensions, including the human resources.

Implementation of Basel II required closer cooperation, information sharing and co-ordination of policies among sectoral supervisors, especially in the context of financial conglomerates.

5.3.6 Basel III Norms in India: Capital Regulations: As per the circular issued by the Reserve Bank of India on March 27, 2014, it was stated that, "in view of the implementation of Basel III Capital Regulations, banks need to improve and strengthen their capital planning processes. While conducting the capital planning exercise, banks may consider the potential impact of the changing macro-economic conditions and the outcomes of periodic stress tests on the adequacy and composition of regulatory capital.

The capital requirements may be substantially lower during the initial years as compared to later years of full implementation of Basel III Guidelines. Accordingly, banks should keep this aspect in view while undertaking their capital planning exercise".

In terms of Basel III Capital Regulations issued by the Reserve Bank of India, the Capital Conservation Buffer (CCB) was scheduled to be implemented from March 31, 2015 in phases and to be fully implemented by March 31, 2018. However, it was decided that the implementation of CCB will begin as on March 31, 2016. Consequently, Basel III Capital Regulations were to be fully implemented as on March 31, 2019. However, RBI has given an extension of a year till March 31, 2020 for the implementation of last tranche of CCB.

Implementation of Basel III framework will throw various challenges for Indian banks. The adoption of Basel III capital requirements by Indian banks would push down their return on equity (RoE) to an extent.

5.4 Challenges for the Banking Sector

Banking system in India has undergone significant transformation following financial sector reforms since the early 1990s. The thrust of the banking sector reforms was on increasing operational efficiency, strengthening the prudential and supervisory norms, removing external constraints, creating competitive conditions and developing the technological and institutional infrastructure. The impact of the reform measures is reflected in an improvement in profitability, financial health, soundness and overall efficiency of the banking sector. Banks have been able to maintain or increase their capital adequacy ratio, despite the sharp increase in their risk-weighted assets.

The Indian banking system is currently passing through a crucial phase. Although the banking sector has become strong, competitive, dynamic and resilient, it is faced with several newer challenges as a result of macroeconomic and financial sector developments, both domestic and global. The major issues/challenges faced by the Indian banking sector could be identified as follows:

1. Emergence of financial conglomerates, which has raised the issue of appropriate regulatory structure/arrangement.
2. Emergence of complex financial products, which pose several supervisory challenges.
3. Need to extend financial services to the large number of people who continue to remain outside the banking system.
4. Mobilising resources to sustain and even accelerate the current economic growth momentum.
5. Issues involved in allowing increased presence of foreign banks in India as the roadmap for foreign banks.
6. Progressive move towards fuller capital account convertibility, which will expose the banking system to greater risks and would require addressing certain issues in banking, including some regulatory and supervisory aspects.

In the banking industry, it is fast changing the way products are conceived, designed and delivered across channels and market segments. Today, technology enabled business models are disrupting the entire supply chain be it retail, corporate or government business. The emergence of third party aggregators for loans, personal finance management, rural banking products/services, payments etc. are making significant impact to our traditional business processes or models.

With increasing adoption of technologies like mobility, cloud, social media, electronically transferable database etc., technology will continue to be critical in responding to customer expectations across identified market segments and creating the agility needed to respond to opportunities. In order to derive a competitive advantage, banks must therefore effectively leverage technology to deliver on fast-changing customer expectations, align with regulatory controls and compliances, and attract the tech-savvy Generation Y.

It is, therefore, critical for banks to increase their IT investments to align with new innovations in technology to meet their objectives. In this context, technology initiatives in the banking industry coupled with continued innovations by technology vendors will define a new growth path for the industry. In addition to IT innovations and applications, banks are also leveraging social media to reach out to the next generation.

6

Payment Banks

On September 23, 2013, Committee on Comprehensive Financial Services for Small Businesses and Low Income Households (Chairman: Nachiket Mor), was formed by the Reserve Bank of India (RBI). On January 7, 2014, the Committee submitted its final report. Among its various recommendations, it recommended the formation of a new category of banks called payment banks. On July 17, 2014, the RBI released the draft guidelines for payment banks, seeking comments for interested entities and the general public. On November 27, 2014 the RBI released the final guidelines for payment banks.

It may be recalled that in the Union Budget 2014-2015 presented on July 10, 2014, the Finance Minister had announced, "After making suitable changes to current framework, a structure will be put in place for continuous authorization of universal banks in the private sector in the current financial year. RBI will create a framework for licensing small banks and other differentiated banks. Differentiated banks serving niche interests, local area banks, payment banks etc. are contemplated to meet credit and remittance needs of small businesses, unorganized sector, low income households, farmers and migrant work force".

6.1 Guidelines for Licensing of Payment Banks

RBI released on November 27, 2014 the following guidelines for licensing of payments banks.

6.1.1 Objective: The objective of setting up of payments banks is to further financial inclusion by providing: (a) small savings accounts and (b) payments/remittance services to migrant labour workforce, low income households, small businesses, other unorganised sector entities and other users.

6.1.2 Eligible Promoters: Existing non-bank pre-paid payment instrument (PPI) issuers and other entities—such as individuals/professionals, non-banking finance companies (NBFCs), corporate business correspondents (BCs), mobile telephone companies, super-market chains, companies, real sector cooperatives—that are owned and controlled by residents; and public sector entities may apply to set up payments banks.

A promoter/promoter group can have a joint venture with an existing scheduled commercial bank to set up a payments bank. However, scheduled commercial bank can take equity stake in a payments bank to the extent permitted under Section 19(2) of the Banking Regulation Act, 1949.

Promoter/promoter groups should be *fit and proper* with a sound track record of professional experience or running their businesses for at least a period of 5 years in order to be eligible to promote payments banks.

6.1.3 Scope of Activities: As regards acceptance of demand deposits, payment banks will initially be restricted to holding a maximum balance of ₹ 1,00,000 per individual customer. However, it may be raised by the RBI based on the performance of the bank.

Payments banks cannot issue credit cards. Payments and remittance services will be provided through various channels.

25 percent of the branches of a payment bank must be in the unbanked rural area. The bank must use the term *payments bank* to differentiate it from other types of banks. The bank will be licensed as payments bank under Section 22 of the Banking Regulation Act, 1949 and will be registered as a public limited company under the Companies Act, 2013.

6.1.4 Deployment of Funds: Payment banks cannot undertake lending activities. Apart from amounts maintained as cash reserve ratio (CRR) with the RBI on its outside demand and time liabilities, payment banks will be required to invest minimum 75 percent of their *demand deposit balances* in statutory liquidity ratio (SLR) eligible Government securities/treasury bills with maturity up to 1 year and hold maximum 25 percent in current and time/fixed deposits with other scheduled commercial banks for operational purposes and liquidity management.

6.1.5 Capital Requirement: The minimum paid-up equity capital for payment banks is ₹ 100 crore. Payments banks should have a leverage ratio of not less than 3 percent, i.e. their outside liabilities should not exceed 33.33 times their net worth (paid-up capital and reserves).

6.1.6 Promoter's Contribution: Promoter's minimum initial contribution to the paid-up equity capital of such payment banks shall, at least, be 40 percent for the first five years from the commencement of the business.

6.1.7 Foreign Shareholding: Foreign shareholding in the payment banks would be as per the foreign direct investment (FDI) policy for private sector banks as amended from time to time.

6.1.8 Voting Rights: The voting rights will be regulated by the Banking Regulation Act, 1949. The voting right of any shareholder is capped at 10 percent, which can be raised to 26 percent by RBI. Any acquisition of more than 5 percent will require approval of the RBI. The majority of the bank's board of director should consist of independent directors, appointed according to RBI guidelines.

6.1.9 Other Conditions: Operations of the bank should be fully networked and technology driven from the beginning, conforming to generally accepted standards and norms. The bank can accept utility bills. It cannot form subsidiaries to undertake non-banking activities. The bank should have a high powered customer grievances cell to handle customer complaints.

6.1.10 Procedure for Application: In terms of Rule 11 of the Banking Regulation (Companies) Rules, 1949, applications shall be submitted in the prescribed form (Form III) to the Chief General Manager, Department of Banking Regulation, Reserve Bank of India, Mumbai. In addition, the applicants should furnish the business plan and other requisite information as indicated. Applications will be accepted till the close of business as on January 16, 2015. After experience gained in dealing with payments banks, applications will be received on a continuous basis. However, these guidelines are subject to periodic review and revision.

6.1.11 Procedure for RBI Decisions: An External Advisory Committee (EAC) comprising eminent professionals like bankers, chartered accountants, finance professionals etc. will evaluate the applications. The decision to issue an in-principle approval for setting up of a bank will be taken by the RBI. Decision of the RBI in this regard will be final.

The validity of the in-principle approval issued by the RBI will be 18 months. The names of applicants for bank licences will be placed on the website of RBI.

In February 2015, RBI released the list of entities which had applied for a payment bank licence. There were 41 applicants. It was also announced that an external advisory committee (EAC) headed by Nachiket Mor would evaluate the licence applications.

EAC submitted its findings on July 6, 2015. The applicant entities were examined for their financial track record and governance issues. On August 19, 2015, the RBI gave *in-principle* licences to the following 11 entities to launch payment banks:

1. Aditya Birla Nuvo.
2. Airtel M Commerce Services.
3. Cholamandalam Distribution Services.
4. Department of Posts.
5. FINO PayTech.
6. National Securities Depository.
7. Reliance Industries.
8. Dilip Shanghvi, Sun Pharmaceuticals.
9. Vijay Shekhar Sharma, Paytm.
10. Tech Mahindra.
11. Vodafone M-Pesa.

The *in-principle* license was valid for 18 months within

which the entities were to fulfil the requirements. They were not allowed to engage in banking activities within the period. The RBI would consider grant of full licenses under Section 22 of the Banking Regulation Act, 1949, after it was satisfied that the conditions had been fulfilled.

On February 28, 2015, during the presentation of the Union Budget it was announced that India Post [1] will use its large network to run payment banks. On June 1, 2016, Union Cabinet cleared the proposal to set up postal payment banks. There are 1,54,000 post offices in the country out of which 1,39,000 are in rural areas. 650 branches of postal payment banks will be established in the country and linked to rural post offices. By September 2017, all 650 branches of postal payment banks will become operational.

Thus, payment bank is a new model of banks conceptualised by the Reserve Bank of India (RBI). These banks can accept a restricted deposit, which is currently limited to ₹ 1 lakh per customer and may be increased further. These banks cannot issue loans and credit cards. Both current account and savings accounts can be operated by such banks. Payments banks can issue services like ATM cards, debit cards, net-banking and mobile-banking. Bharti Airtel set up India's first live payments bank.

According to RBI, the objective of setting up of payment banks is to further financial inclusion by providing: (a) small savings accounts and (b) payments/remittance services to migrant labour workforce, low income households, small businesses, other unorganised sector entities and other user.

6.2 India Post Payments Bank (IPPB)

IPPB operates under the Department of Posts, Ministry of Communications, Government of India. It aims to utilize all of India’s 1,55,015 post offices as access points and 3,00,000 postal service workers to provide house-to-house banking services. The first phase of the bank with 650 branches and 3,250 post offices as access points was inaugurated on September 1, 2018 by Prime

Minister Shri Narendra Modi. Over 10,000 postmen have been roped into the first phase.

On August 19, 2015, India Post got licence to run a payment bank from Reserve Bank of India. On August 17, 2016, it was registered as a public limited government company for setting up a payment bank. The pilot project of IPPB was inaugurated on January 30, 2017 at Raipur and Ranchi. In August 2018, the Union Cabinet approved ₹ 1,435 crore for setting up the bank. The first phase nationwide inauguration happened on September 1, 2018.

IPPB offers savings accounts, money transfer and insurances through third parties, bill and utility payments. It will reach to rural and far-flung areas of the country, delivering banking services to the doorstep of every Indian.

- The bank offers savings and current accounts up to a balance of ₹ 1 lakh.
- Customers can use QR code payments eliminating the need to remember account numbers, PINs and passwords.
- Unified payments interface.
- Immediate payment service.
- National electronic funds transfer.
- Real-time gross settlement.
- Bharat BillPay.
- Direct benefit transfer.

IPPB has been allowed to link around 17 crore postal savings bank (PSB) accounts with its accounts. The Government aims to link all the 1,55,000 post offices to the IPPB system by December 31, 2018.

IPPB will use Aadhaar to open accounts, while a QR card and biometrics will drive authentication, transactions, and payments.

The Government owns 100 percent in IPPB, which has been set up under the aegis of the Department of Posts, and will offer products and services though multiple channels such as counter services, micro ATMs, mobile banking app, messages and interactive voice response.

6.2.1 Main Features of IPPB: These are as under:

1. *Grameen Dak Sewaks* will be armed with smart phones and biometric devices to handle transactions.
2. IPPB will operate like a banking organisation, but with smaller scale operations. Most banking operations like accepting deposits shall be done, but loans cannot be given and credit cards cannot be issued.
3. IPPB can accept deposits of up to ₹ 1 lakh per customer, offer payments and remittance services, mobile payments/transfers/purchases and other banking services like ATM/debit cards, net banking and third-party fund transfers.
4. IPPB has tied-up with PNB and Bajaj Allianz Life Insurance for products such as loans as well as insurance. These facilities can be accessed through 650 branches and 3,250 access points.
5. Around 1,30,000 access points will be located in rural areas to fulfil Government's financial inclusion goal. IPPB also has a nod to link around 17 crore postal savings bank (PSB) accounts with its own set-up.
6. Deposits in any account that exceed ₹ 1 lakh will be automatically converted into post office savings account.
7. IPPB will give different interest rate according to the deposit amount.

- Deposit up to ₹ 25,000—4.5 percent
- Deposit up to ₹ 50,000—5 percent
- Up to ₹ 1,00,000—5.5 percent

8. One can open a zero balance saving account.
9. Existing saving account with the post offices can be converted into IPPB saving account. It would give a better interest rate.
10. Government is planning to send postman to your home for cash deposit and withdrawals. It would be a charged service.

6.3 Other Prominent Payment Banks in India

6.3.1 Airtel Payment Bank: It is a public limited company with its headquarters in New Delhi. The company is a subsidiary of Bharti Airtel. It is the first company in India to receive a payments bank license from RBI and it became the first live payments bank in the country. On April 11, 2016, RBI issued the license under Section 22(1) of Banking Regulation Act, 1949 to Airtel Payment Bank. It is a joint venture between Bharti Airtel Ltd. and Kotak Mahindra Bank Ltd. Kotak Mahindra Bank holds 19.9 percent stake in the Airtel Payment Bank.

Main features of Airtel Payment Bank are as under:

- The bank supports UPI payment system for fund transfer. The UPI is the most advanced mechanism of fund transfer. It is free, instant and always available.
- It gives a free digital debit card in association with the MasterCard. There is an annual charge for this card.
- The bank opens your account instantly and requires no documents. It only needs your Aadhaar along with the fingerprints.
- Your Airtel number is your bank account number.
- Free Personal Accident Insurance cover of ₹ 1 lakh.

6.3.2 Paytm Payment Bank: Paytm is promoting its payment bank and advising its wallet customers to shift into the payment bank. The bank started its operation in December 2017.

Some features of Paytm Payment Bank are as under:

- It opens a zero balance account.
- Free insurance cover of ₹ 2 lakh.
- Fixed deposit facility in partnership with IndusInd Bank.
- Free Digital Rupay Debit card.

6.3.3 Fino Payment Bank: Fino Payment Bank has not advertised itself much but it has a strong footing. This bank gives a variety of services which include current and savings accounts, remittances, business correspondent (BC) lending, mobile banking, life and general insurance and bill payments.

Important features of Fino Payment Bank are as follows:

- It has its own branches at 410 places.
- It is present at BPCL petrol pumps.
- The bank has focussed on remittance business.

- It has partnered with the ICICI Bank. ICICI ATMs are installed at Fino branches.
- It also sells auto loans, personal loans and home loans of the ICICI Bank.
- The bank requires ₹ 1,000 minimum balance in the account.

6.3.4 Aditya Birla Idea Payment Bank: The bank started operations from February 22, 2018. However, the details are not out yet. Similarly, Jio Payment Bank is also in the process of establishing itself.

Though not a payment bank, Google Pay (formerly Google Tez) is an online payment app that provides users with an option to send or receive money over Unified Payments Interface (UPI). Unlike traditional payment transfer methods like NEFT and RTGS, UPI makes it easier to send or receive money directly from or to a bank account in real time, just like a text message.

Endnote

1. Department of Posts (India Post) is a department of the Ministry of Communications and Information Technology, Government of India. Postal services in India have touched the lives of every citizen for more than 150 years, be it through mails, banking, insurance, money transfer or retail services.

7

Foreign Banks in India

For financial institutions to operate efficiently, there is a need to maintain competitive conditions. The empirical and theoretical literature in banking also suggests that a competitive banking system is more efficient. It has therefore, been the endeavour of the Government and the Reserve Bank of India (RBI) to enhance competition through entry of new private sector banks, increased presence of foreign banks and provision of operational flexibility to public sector banks. To diversify ownership, public sector banks were allowed to raise funds from the capital markets, subject to the Government shareholding being retained at 51 percent. Various other restrictions hindering the competitive process have also been, by and large, phased out. As on January 31, 2018, there were 45 foreign banks operating in India with 286 branches.

7.1 Emergence of Foreign Banks

In recognition of the emergence of foreign banks as key vehicles in the international integration of the financial systems, a liberalised policy towards foreign banks' entry has become a high priority in policymakers' agenda in various countries in recent years. Liberalisation of financial services by allowing foreign financial institutions to participate in the domestic market improves competition, thereby facilitating better and cheaper financial intermediation. Apart from increasing competition and efficiency through infusion of technology and skill management, some of the other benefits of foreign banks' entry are said to include introduction of superior risk management practices and stronger capital base, which is also less sensitive to host country's business cycle.

India also liberalised the entry of foreign banks in the post-reform period. In the roadmap by the RBI released in February 2005, the opening up of the domestic banking sector to foreign banks was envisioned in two phases. The first phase envisaged that foreign banks wishing to establish presence in India for the first time could either choose to operate through branch presence or set up a 100 percent wholly-owned subsidiary (WOS) following the one-mode presence criterion. In the second phase (April 2009 onwards), the policy on foreign banks is to be taken up for a review. At that stage, various issues associated with the increased presence of foreign banks such as impact on the domestic banks, supervisory and regulatory challenges in view of their sophisticated operations and their involvement in complex and sophisticated products, financial inclusion, credit to agriculture and SMEs, and public policy on credit delivery, cost and allocation would need to be weighed. The issues relating to co-ordination between home and host countries regulators would also pose a challenge.

RBI released the framework for setting up of wholly owned subsidiaries (WOS) by foreign banks in India on November 6, 2013. The policy framework is guided by the two cardinal principles of reciprocity and single mode of presence. As a locally incorporated bank, the WOSs will be given near national treatment which will enable them to open branches anywhere in the country at par with Indian banks (except in certain sensitive areas where the Reserve Bank's prior approval would be required). The policy incentivises the existing foreign bank branches to convert into WOS due to the attractiveness of near national treatment. Such conversion is also desirable from the financial stability perspective, factoring in the lessons from the global economic crisis.

7.2 Advantages of Foreign Banks

The following are the commonly highlighted benefits of foreign bank entry.

First, it heightens competition and promotes efficiency leading to decline in costs or increase in productivity. When a foreign bank enters through greenfield investment and sets up a *de novo* institution, the increase in the number of banks in the host country directly enhances competition. Entry through merger and acquisition, which infuses more skilled management and upgrade governance through introducing more advanced systems and risk management, may force other banks in the host country to improve their efficiency in order to protect their market shares.

Second, entry of foreign banks improves credit allocation, as in making credit decisions, they apply formal credit standards and risk-adjusted pricing and are not influenced by other considerations.

Third, foreign banks help in the development of local financial markets since they have both the incentives and the expertise to develop certain segments of local market, such as funding, derivatives and securities markets. Foreign banks that lack a branch network to guarantee deposit financing of their activities are more likely to turn to the inter-bank market. Foreign banks can also contribute by bringing professional expertise to the local foreign currency markets. They often try to create markets or gain market share through product innovation, especially by offering a variety of new financial services to corporate clients, including structured products.

Fourth, the overall soundness of domestic financial system is enhanced by introducing the risk management practices of the foreign parent banks. Based on tighter credit review policies and practices, they adopt more aggressive measures to address asset quality deterioration and limit the build-up of non-performing assets in the financial system.

Fifth, foreign banks may exert a stabilising influence in times of financial distress, as stronger capitalisation and the possibility of an injection of additional funds by the parent, if needed, reduces the probability of failure. For the same, foreign banks are less sensitive to both home and host country business cycles, and consequently, lending to local residents in the local market is likely to be more stable in times of stress than either cross-border lending or the lending of indigenous banks in the markets. Further, when the foreign banks continue to operate in a crisis, the probability of the system as a whole remaining functional, increases.

Sixth, there could be long-term benefits from lower cost structures in the banking system. Foreign banks, in general, are found to operate with lower administrative costs as has been found in Latin America and most of other developing countries. However, in some countries such as India, operating cost of foreign banks was found to be higher than that of domestic banks.

Seventh, foreign ownership usually involves the transfer of human capital at both the managerial and the operational level. Complementary to this is the transfer of *soft* infrastructure such as back office routines or credit control systems. Such transfers have gained importance to reap economies of scale through standardisation of processes.

7.3 Disadvantages of Foreign Banks

There could also be several costs associated with the entry of foreign banks.

First, entry of foreign banks could also lead to concentration and loss of competition. In many countries, foreign banks entered the system mainly by acquiring existing domestic banks, while in some countries domestic banks consolidation and concentration occurred in response to foreign competition.

Second, though foreign banks entry may lower interest margins and potentially foster the process of financial intermediation, the impact would depend on the form it takes and may not benefit all borrowers. The benefits would depend on whether the lower spread is the result of a more aggressive pricing strategy across the board or the banks choosing to lend only to the most transparent segments where there is more competition or at least greater market contestability.

Third, the growing presence of foreign banks can increase the complexity of the tasks facing supervisory authorities and thus lead to regulatory conflicts. This could be a particular concern in countries where foreign commercial banks expand their operations rapidly in the area of non-bank financial services such as insurance, portfolio management, and investment banking. Given the complex structure of many internationally active banks, integral issues within foreign banks are increasingly being shown to be of potential systemic significance.

Fourth, foreign banks expose the country to some downside risks/challenges attached with their entry. More strikingly, domestic banks in emerging markets generally incur costs since they have to compete with large international banks with better reputation, particularly in developing world.

Fifth, there is a general concern that as foreign banks have historically followed home-country customers or specialised in servicing corporate customers, their entry would lead to neglect of rural customers and small and medium sized firms. Another concern is that with foreign banks using the inter-bank market for much of their funding, local banks could divert their funds from domestic loans to the inter-bank market, thereby channelling fund to large corporate at the expense of small companies.

Sixth, it is also argued that the presence of foreign banks may not necessarily yield a more stable source of credit to domestic borrowers because foreign banks can, at times, shift funds abruptly from one market to another for risk management purposes. Literature also suggests that foreign banks will be more likely to shift their funds to more attractive markets during a crisis if their parent banks are weak.

Table 7.1 provides the list of foreign banks in India.

Table 7.2 provides a list of top 10 foreign banks in India.

7.4 Road Map for Foreign Banks in India

With a view to delineate the direction and pace of reform process in this area and to operationalise the extant guidelines of March 4, 2004 in a phased manner, the RBI, on February 28, 2005, released the road map for presence of foreign banks in India. The roadmap was divided into two phases.

Table 7.1: List of Foreign Banks in India
(As on January 31, 2018)

1.	AB Bank Ltd.	24.	Industrial and Commercial Bank of China Ltd.
2.	Abu Dhabi Commercial Bank Ltd.	25.	JP Morgan Chase Bank N.A.
3.	American Express Banking Corporation	26.	JSC VTB Bank
4.	Australia and New Zealand Banking Group Ltd.	27.	Krung Thai Bank Public Co. Ltd
5.	BNP Paribas	28.	KEB Hana bank
6.	Bank of America	29.	Mashreq Bank PSC
7.	Bank of Bahrain and Kuwait BSC	30.	Mizuho Bank Ltd.
8.	Bank of Ceylon	31.	National Australia Bank
9.	Bank of Nova Scotia	32.	PT Bank Maybank Indonesia TBK
10.	Barclays Bank Plc	33.	Qatar National Bank
11.	CTBC Bank Co. Ltd.	34.	SBM Bank (Mauritius) Ltd.
12.	Citibank N.A.	35.	Sberbank
13.	Cooperative Rabobank U.A.	36.	Societe Generale
14.	Credit Agricole Corporate and Investment Bank	37.	Shinhan Bank
15.	Credit Suisse A.G.	38.	Sonali Bank
16.	DBS Bank Ltd.	39.	Standard Chartered Bank
17.	Deutsche Bank	40.	Sumitomo Mitsui Banking Corporation
18.	Doha Bank	41.	The Bank of Tokyo-Mitsubishi UFJ Ltd.
19.	Emirates bank NBD	42.	The Royal Bank of Scotland Plc
20.	First Abu Dhabi Bank PJSC	43.	Westpac Banking Corporation
21.	FirstRand Bank Ltd.	44.	United Overseas Bank Ltd.
22.	HSBC Ltd.	45.	Woori Bank
23.	Industrial Bank of Korea		

Source: Reserve Bank of India.

7.4.1 Phase I: March 2005 to March 2009: During the first phase, foreign banks were permitted to establish presence by way of setting up a wholly-owned banking subsidiary (WOS) or conversion of the existing branches into a WOS. The guidelines covered, *inter alia*, the eligibility criteria of the applicant foreign banks such as ownership pattern, financial soundness, supervisory rating and the international ranking. The WOS was required to have a minimum capital requirement of ₹ 300 crore and maintain a capital adequacy ratio of 10 percent or as was prescribed from time to time on a continuous basis, from the commencement of its operations.

Table 7.2: Top 10 Foreign Banks in India and their Branches (as on January 31, 2018)

S. No.	Name of the Bank	Number of Branches in India
1.	Standard Chartered Bank	100
2.	Citibank N.A.	35
3.	HSBC Ltd.	26
4.	Deutsche Bank	17
5.	DBS Bank Ltd.	12
6.	BNP Paribas	8
7.	Barclays Bank PLC	6
8.	Shinhan bank	6
9.	Credit Agricole Corporate and Investment Bank	5
10.	Mizuho Bank Ltd.	5

Source: Reserve Bank of India.

The WOS was treated on par with the existing branches of foreign banks for branch expansion with flexibility to go beyond the existing WTO commitments of 12 branches in a year and preference for branch expansion in under-banked areas. During this phase, permission for acquisition of share holding in Indian private sector banks by eligible foreign banks was limited to banks identified by the RBI for restructuring. The RBI—if it was satisfied that such investment by the foreign bank concerned was in the long-term interest of all the stakeholders in the investee bank—permitted such acquisition. Where such acquisition was by a foreign bank having presence in India, a maximum period of 6 months was given for conforming to the *one form of presence* concept.

7.4.2 Phase II: April 2009 onward: Phase II commenced in April 2009 after a review of the experience gained and after due consultation with all the stakeholders in the banking sector. The review examined issues concerning extension of national treatment to WOS, dilution of stake and permitting mergers/acquisitions of any private sector banks in India by a foreign bank in Phase II.

The parent foreign bank will continue to hold 100 percent equity in the Indian subsidiary for a minimum prescribed period of operation. The composition of the board of directors should, *inter alia*, meet the following requirements: (a) not less than 50 percent of the directors should be Indian nationals resident in India, and (b) not less than 50 percent of the directors should be non-executive directors.

Foreign banks which commenced banking business in India before August 2010 shad the option to continue their banking business through the branch mode. However, they were incentivised to convert into WOS. To prevent domination by foreign banks, restrictions would be placed on further entry of new WOSs of foreign banks/capital infusion, when the capital and reserves of the WOSs and foreign bank branches in India exceed 20 percent of the capital and reserves of the banking system. The initial minimum paid-up voting equity capital for a WOS shall be ₹ 5 billion for new entrants.

8

Urban Co-operative Banks (UCBs)

Financial sector reforms have been components of the overall economic reforms undertaken in a phased manner from 1991 by the Government of India. A look has to be taken at the reform process and what it means to the co-operative credit institutions. These reforms also envisaged improving the efficiency and productivity of the co-operative credit delivery system which in turn would accelerate the requisite credit flow to the productive sectors of the economy.

The major objectives of these reforms in the co-operative sector were as under:

1. To make the institutions competitive by removing external constraints having a bearing on their operations.
2. To improve their financial health.
3. To ensure transparency in their business operations.
4. To improve their profitability.
5. Institutional building and strengthening.

It is significant to note that introduction of reforms and the consequent increase in competition has resulted in some convergence in operations of commercial banks and co-operative banks, especially scheduled UCBs. Furthermore, while most of the loss-making commercial banks are relatively small, in the case of UCBs some of the large banks are incurring losses and this has increased the vulnerability of the whole segment. Detection of irregularities in a few UCBs in the recent past has raised concerns about the conduct of the management in co-operative banks. For this purpose, the RBI has suggested the establishment of a unified supervisory authority for UCBs and the related amendment to the Banking Regulation Act, 1949.

8.1 Importance of UCBs

The co-operative banking system forms an integral part of the Indian financial system. It comprises urban cooperative banks and rural co-operative credit institutions. Urban co-operative banks (UCBs) have a single-tier structure whereas rural co-operatives have a two- or three-tier structure. As on May 29, 2019, there were 1,488 non-scheduled UCBs in India.

The single-tier urban co-operative banks (UCBs)—also referred to as primary cooperative banks—play an important role in meeting the growing credit needs of urban and semi-urban areas of the country. The UCBs, which grew rapidly in the early 1990s, showed certain weaknesses arising out of lack of sound corporate governance, unethical lending, comparatively high levels of non-performing loans and their inability to operate in a liberalised environment. Accordingly, some of the weak UCBs have been either liquidated or merged with other banks.

Co-operative banks in India are more than 100 years old. These banks came into existence with the enactment of the Agricultural Credit Co-operative Societies Act in 1904. Co-operative banks form an integral part of the banking system in India. These banks operate mainly for the benefit of rural areas, particularly the agricultural sector. Co-operative banks mobilise deposits and supply agricultural and rural credit with a wider outreach. They are the main source of institutional credit to the farmers. Co-operative banks are chiefly responsible for breaking the monopoly of moneylenders in providing credit to agriculturists. They have also been an important instrument for various development schemes, particularly subsidy-based programmes for the poor. Co-operative banks operate for non-agricultural sector also but their role is small.

Though much smaller as compared to scheduled commercial banks, co-operative banks constitute an important segment of the Indian banking system. They have an extensive branch network and reach out to people in remote areas. They have traditionally played an important role in creating banking habits among the lower and middle-income groups and in strengthening the rural credit delivery system.

Urban co-operative banks play an important role in meeting the growing credit needs of urban and semi-urban areas. UCBs mobilise savings from the middle and lower income groups and purvey credit to small borrowers, including weaker sections of the society. Scheduled UCBs are under closer regulatory and supervisory framework of the RBI.

The financial reforms process initiated in 1991 has tried to achieve regulatory convergence among various financial intermediaries in view of their systemic importance. Therefore, the basic objectives and instruments of reforms for co-operative banks have been the same as for state co-operative banks (SCBs). However, given the special characteristics of co-operative banks, they have been extended certain dispensations in terms of pace and sequencing of reforms.

UCBs have grown rapidly since the early 1990s. During the phase of rapid expansion, however, the sector showed certain weaknesses arising out of: (a) lack of sound corporate governance, (b) unethical lending, (c) comparatively high level of loan defaults, and (d) inability to operate in a liberalised and competitive environment. The RBI, therefore, has been striving to harness the growth of UCBs with appropriate application of prudential regulation and supervision to safeguard the interests of depositors.

Keeping in view the weak financial position of many UCBs, the RBI has undertaken a series of measures directed towards strengthening of the UCBs. Since March 31, 1993, the UCBs have been advised to adhere to the prudential norms which include, *inter alia*, the following.

1. Applying capital adequacy standards.
2. Prescribing an asset-liability management framework.
3. Enhancing the proportion of holding of Government and other approved securities for the purpose of statutory liquidity ratio (SLR) stipulation.
4. Restriction on bank finance against the security of corporate shares and debentures.

5. Limiting the exposure to capital market investment.

In view of the challenges arising from the functioning of the UCBs for the financial system, the RBI appointed a High Power Committee (Chairman: K. Madhava Rao), 1999 to review the performance of UCBs and to suggest necessary measures to strengthen this sector. Based on the recommendations of this Committee, measures have been initiated to strengthen the existing urban banking structure.

8.2 Vision Document and Medium-Term Framework (MTF) for UCBs

Various entities in the urban co-operative banking sector display a high degree of heterogeneity in terms of deposits and asset base, areas of operation and nature of business. In view of its importance, it is imperative that the sector emerges as a sound and healthy network of jointly owned, democratically controlled and professionally managed institutions. In order to achieve these objectives, the RBI has taken a series of policy initiatives in recent years. The most significant initiative in this regard was the Vision Document and Medium-Term Framework (MTF) for UCBs released in 2005. With a view to protecting depositors' interests on the one hand, and enabling UCBs to provide useful service to local communities on the other, the medium-term framework (MTF) seeks to achieve the following objectives.

1. To rationalise the existing regulatory and supervisory approach keeping in view the heterogeneous character of the entities in the sector.
2. To facilitate a focused and continuous system of supervision through enhancement of technology.
3. To enhance professionalism and improve the quality of governance in UCBs by providing training for skill upgradation and also by including large depositors in the decision making process/management of banks.
4. To put in place a mechanism that addresses the problems of dual control, given the present legal framework and the

time-consuming process in bringing requisite legislative changes.

5. To put in place a consultative arrangement for identifying weak but potentially viable entities in the sector and provide a framework for nursing them back to health including, if necessary, through a process of consolidation.
6. To identify the unviable entities in the sector and provide an exit route for such entities.

The above framework is implemented through the following measures:

1. A differentiated regulatory regime as opposed to a *one-size-fits-all* approach.
2. A two-tier regulatory regime: (a) simplified regulatory regime for unit banks and single district banks with deposits less than ₹ 100 crore, and (b) regulation for all other banks on the lines of commercial banks.
3. As the strategy to deal with UCBs may need to be State-specific, a State Level Task Force for Urban Co-operative Banks (TAFCUB) is to be constituted comprising senior officials from the RBI, State Governments and local/central co-operative Federations.
4. TAFCUB would be responsible for: (i) identifying weak but viable UCBs and devise a time-bound programme for revival; and (ii) recommending: (a) the nature and extent of financial support, (b) future set up of unlicensed banks, and (c) the manner and timeframe for exit of unviable banks.
5. To address issues/difficulties relating to dual control within the existing legal framework, it has been proposed to evolve a working arrangement in the form of memorandum of understanding (MoU) between the RBI and the State Government.

8.3 Regulation and Supervision of UCBs

The regulation and supervision of the urban co-operative banks (UCBs) was brought within the ambit of the RBI's statutory control under the Banking Laws (as Applicable to Cooperative Societies) Act, which came into force from March 1, 1966. The regulatory powers conferred on the RBI with regard to co-operative banks are limited. While the principles of supervision with regard to co-operative banks have been formulated and implemented by the RBI in respect of UCBs under the Banking Regulation Act, 1949, the Act does not apply to primary agricultural credit societies and land development banks, thus leaving them under the regulatory purview of the State.

Instances such as the Madhavapura Mercantile Co-operative Bank's failure brought to the fore the need to have stringent regulatory control over the co-operative banking system. In order to strengthen the supervisory mechanism, the RBI extended the off-site surveillance system (OSS) to all non-scheduled UCBs having deposit size of ₹ 100 crore and above. A supervisory reporting system was introduced for the scheduled UCBs from March 2001 as a first step towards setting up of OSS for all UCBs. The capital adequacy norms were introduced in a phased manner from March 2002. Better risk management through avoidance of concentration of credit risk, off-site surveillance for non-scheduled UCBs and following up of know your customer (KYC) guidelines have also been introduced to strengthen the UCBs.

A total ban has been imposed since October 2003 on grant of loans and advances to directors of UCBs, their relatives and concerns in which they have interest with a view to preventing certain irregularities. The RBI has also directed that UCBs should undertake usual due diligence in respect of investments in non-SLR securities.

RBI introduced a new system of grading of UCBs in April 2003, which is based on their CRAR, level of net NPAs, record of losses and compliance with regulatory environment. Similarly, a system of supervisory rating for UCBs under the CAMELS model has also been introduced. Initially, it was implemented for scheduled UCBs but subsequently its simplified version was extended to non-scheduled UCBs in March 2004.

Despite the structural and cultural differences between UCBs and commercial banks, the above measures suggest that the RBI has been exercising its regulatory and supervisory powers to ensure that the co-operative credit structure is strengthened on the lines similar to the regulation and supervision of commercial banks.

The RBI is entrusted with the responsibility of regulation and supervision of the banking-related activities of UCBs under the Banking Regulation Act, 1949 as Applicable to Co-operative Societies (AACS). Other aspects such as incorporation, registration, administration, management and winding-up of UCBs are supervised and regulated by the respective State Governments through Registrars of Co-operative Societies (RCS) under the Co-operative Societies Acts of the respective States. UCBs with a multi-state presence are registered under the Multi-State Co-operative Societies Act, 2002 and are regulated and supervised jointly by the Central Government through Central Registrar of Co-operative Societies and the RBI.

Thus, current legislative framework provides for dual control over UCBs. For resolving problems arising out of dual control regime, a draft legislative bill proposing certain amendments to the Banking Regulation Act, 1949 (AACS), based on the recommendations of the High Powered Committee on UCBs, was forwarded to the Government. Pending the amendment to the Act, the RBI is entering into a regulatory arrangement with the State Governments through memorandum of understanding (MoU) to facilitate proper and coordinated regulation and supervision of UCBs. MoUs have already been signed between the RBI and three States that have a large network of UCBs, viz. Andhra Pradesh, Gujarat and Karnataka. As a follow-up to the signing of MoUs, the RBI has constituted State Level Task Force for Urban Co-operative Banks (TAFCUBs) in these States.

8.4 IT Support for Urban Co-operative Banks

In today's financial systems, usage of information

technology is fundamental to the survival and growth of the institutions. Current regulatory and supervisory compliance demands that the institutions have a very sound usage of IT systems for their operations.

The Vision Document for Urban Cooperative Banks (UCBs), released in March 2005, proposed signing of memorandum of understanding (MoU) between RBI and Central and respective State governments for establishing a consultative approach to supervision and regulation of UCBs. The Reserve Bank signed such MoUs with 16 State Governments and the Central Government.

In terms of the MoUs, the RBI is committed to facilitate IT initiatives in UCBs. In furtherance of the commitment made under the MoUs, Governor announced in the Mid-term Review of the Annual Policy 2007-08, that 'a working group comprising representatives of the Reserve Bank, State Governments and the UCBs sector' would be constituted 'to examine the various areas where IT support could be provided by the Reserve Bank'. Accordingly, the RBI constituted a Working Group on IT Support for Urban Cooperative Banks (Chairman: R. Gandhi) on December 19, 2007 with the following terms of reference:

1. To review the current level and use of IT infrastructure in UCBs.
2. To structure a model/benchmark level of IT infrastructure for UCBs in general or for identified sub-groups of UCBs.
3. To prepare a roadmap of building such an infrastructure by the UCBs.
4. To identify areas and ways in which IT support may be provided by the RBI.
5. To make recommendations on the nature, scope and delivery mechanism for IT support to UCBs by the RBI.

8.4.1 Findings of the Working Group: There exists a wide disparity with regard to the usage of information technology by the urban co-operative banks. As on March 31, 2007, 16 out of 1853 banks had implemented core banking solutions, while about 50 banks did not even have computers.

The remaining banks exist somewhere along the continuum between those that had CBS on the one hand, and those without even PCs on the other.

Most banks have solutions based on total branch automation. Several banks have implemented locally developed and customised application solutions. While some big UCBs have in-house IT wings to take care of development and maintenance of systems, most banks have outsourced these services.

Anecdotal evidences are there about the problems faced by these banks because of their small size, lack of adequate IT knowledge, lack of adequate IT savvy manpower and small time vendors.

They had suffered because small vendors could not provide satisfactory AMC and adequate post-implementation support for making changes in the software on account of their inability to retain skilled staff or sometimes because of the small scale of their operations, which rendered them unviable. Moreover, such legacy systems, set up by small vendors, were not standardized and therefore made migration to new systems more cumbersome and expensive than even acquiring a new one.

The acquisition of non-standardized software developed by local/regional level vendors is fraught with the following risks:

1. **Vendor Disappearance:** Vendors who developed software for small banks are often small-time operators and are not available for support, modifications and change management subsequently. Their mortality rate is often high. Eventually, the software became obsolete and redundant.
2. **Loss of Key Personnel by Vendor:** Sometimes, the vendor is available but the key personnel, who were involved in the development of software, are no more with the vendor. The vendor finds it difficult to extend the required level of the support without its skilled personnel as being small it has little flexibility in the absence of backup staff. As they often also do not follow standard

practice of software development and documentation, the maintenance and updation of source-codes becomes difficult for the new personnel.

3. **Lack of Regulatory Compliance Modules:** Almost all the small-vendor developed software systems do not contain important regulatory provisions such as compliance to KYC norms etc.

The Group also observed that there were several large banks which had their own data centres and were offering core banking solutions to the smaller banks and that a few successful cases of sharing of data centre facilities among banks were also known. However, as awareness of IT among UCBs was not pervasive, several banks seemed reluctant to keep their data in the data centres owned by other bank/banks.

8.5 Working Group on Umbrella Organization and Revival Fund for Urban Co-operative Banks

There are a large number of urban co-operative banks (UCBs) in the country forming a heterogeneous group in terms of size and spread. Many of these banks are very small in size and reach. They compete with larger participants in the same banking space. Over the years, a number of UCBs have become weak and non-viable thus posing systemic risk to the UCB sector. They lack avenues for raising capital funds since they cannot go in for public issue of shares nor can they issue shares to members at a premium. At the same time, there are a number of UCBs in the sector that are financially strong and viable. Some sort of cooperative bonding and mutual support system could make the sector strong and vibrant. Looking at various successful federal models internationally, especially in Europe and US, a need was felt for an umbrella organization that would be in a position to channelize their resources, aggregate their needs and also lend credibility through mutual support in the financial market.

In this backdrop, RBI constituted a Working Group (Chairman: V.S. Das) on May 28, 2008 to suggest measures including the appropriate regulatory and supervisory framework, to facilitate emergence of umbrella organization(s) for the UCB sector in the respective states. Further, the Standing Advisory Committee for UCBs opined that the Working Group may also look into the issues concerning creation of revival fund for the sector.

8.5.1 Terms of Reference of the Working Group:

1. To study the regulatory and supervisory structure of umbrella organizations of financial co-operative institutions/banks, as prevalent in other parts of the world, especially in relation to raising of capital and intra co-operative group support system.
2. To study the existing structure and legal framework for UCBs in India and to examine the need and scope for a federated structure/umbrella organization for UCBs at the state level.
3. To suggest appropriate supervisory and regulatory framework to facilitate emergence of such umbrella organisation(s) for UCBs, taking into consideration the international experiences and systems.
4. To study and suggest modalities for setting up an appropriate mutual assistance/revival fund for urban co-operative banks and the nature of support that could be provided by such fund.

8.5.2 Recommendations:

A. Need for Umbrella Organization: Urban co-operative banks in India cater to the financial needs of the middle and lower middle class people in metropolitan, urban and semi-urban centres. They operate on a standalone basis, unlike rural cooperatives in India, which have a three tier structure. These banks are large in number, though of varied asset size, ranging from small to medium. Although they compete with commercial banks, their share in total deposits is barely 4 percent. There is a significant part of the UCB sector that lacks professionalism and is unable to keep pace with rapid advancements in IT, modern banking systems and financial products. The sector also has significant number of banks which are weak and need financial support. There have been occasions when, due to contagion effect, banks have encountered liquidity problems. Being in the nature of co-operative societies, the UCBs' ability to augment their capital is also restricted, thereby hindering their growth.

The organizational structure of UCBs, their small size and limited area of operation add to their vulnerability. Further, in the wake of advances in information and communication technology, payment and settlement systems and services, they need to widen their range of services to run on professional lines and match the services provided by commercial banks.

Internationally, cooperative banks, popularly called credit unions, operate in networks and have an entity which provides a wide range of services to them, such as, fund management services, lines of credit, asset management, payment and settlement system gateway, ATM networks, credit card, investment, securitisation, capital raising and other financial services. These entities act as umbrella organizations and the networks provide cooperative solidarity. International experience has shown that the presence of such an umbrella organization has contributed towards the member credit unions being stable, sound and efficient entities.

B. Umbrella Organization at the National Level: The Working Group carefully went into the important issue of whether in India we should have an umbrella organization at the national level or whether each state should have its own umbrella organization. While countries such as Canada and US have provincial umbrella organizations, Australia and European countries have preferred to consolidate and have national level organizations.

UCBs in India are not evenly spread across the country. They have predominant presence in six states, viz. Andhra Pradesh, Gujarat, Karnataka, Maharashtra, Tamil Nadu and Telangana accounting for about 89 percent of the total business of the sector. Further, UCBs in Maharashtra alone had about 64 percent of the total business. In contrast, their presence was minimal in many states. Considering the regional spread and market share of UCBs, the Working Group is of the opinion that having multiple umbrella organizations for UCBs in India or state-wise umbrellas may be neither feasible nor desirable. Therefore, the Working Group recommended that there should be one umbrella organization at the national level for the entire UCB sector.

9

Regional Rural Banks (RRBs)

In spite of the various measures taken by the Government and the RBI through social control and the nationalisation of major commercial banks in 1969, a large proportion of the rural poor remained outside the banking fold. Therefore, the Government of India promoted regional rural banks (RRBs) through the RRBs Act of 1976 to bridge the gap in the flow of credit to the rural poor. The RRBs have a special place in the multi-agency approach adopted to provide agricultural and rural credit in India. These banks are state-sponsored, regionally based and rural-oriented.

The renewed emphasis on agricultural and rural development by the Government of India would lead to a growing demand for different types of financial services in the rural areas, as financial needs of the rural economy becomes diversified. The present structure of rural credit may not be able to cater to the same. RRBs would be called upon to play a greater role in providing such services due to their rural character and feel. RRBs have to take over a larger share of credit disbursements calling for much larger resource mobilization, as also greater efforts for their institutional strengthening.

9.1 Genesis of RRBs

Regional rural banks (RRBs) form an important segment of the rural financial sector. They were conceived as institutions that combine the local feel and familiarity of the co-operatives with the business capabilities of commercial banks. This sector has an exclusive role in improving financial inclusion and catering to vital sectors like agriculture and allied economic activities. Public policy, therefore, aims at keeping this sector viable and strong through various forms of active intervention.

RRBs were introduced and promoted by the Government of India with the noble objective of promoting savings habits and providing credit delivery mechanism to the rural India. The target groups were small and marginal farmers, agricultural labourers, artisans and small entrepreneurs for development of agriculture, trade, industry and other commercial activities in rural India. RRBs have wide reach in rural India and with their region-centric banking activities and closer relationship with the local authorities and population, they were expected to provide necessary banking infrastructure. They have been successful in mobilizing small savings in the rural sector.

Setting up of RRBs in the mid-1970s was a major initiative to meet credit requirements of rural people. The RRBs are specialized rural financial institutions for developing the rural economy by providing credit to small and marginal farmers, agricultural labourers, artisans and small entrepreneurs. During the 40 years of existence of RRBs, several Working Groups and Committees were set up at various points of time to deliberate on issues relating to RRBs and suggest measures to address the same. The focus has varied over time depending on the immediate concerns and the prevailing policy regime. While some of the issues relating to RRBs have lost their significance over time, others have become more relevant.

9.2 Nature and Objectives of RRBs

Agriculture and rural sectors play an important role in India's overall development strategy in terms of income and employment generation and poverty alleviation. Great significance has, therefore, been accorded to developing appropriate institutions and mechanisms for catering to the credit requirements of these sectors.

Despite the measures taken by the Government of India and the RBI—including nationalisation of 14 major commercial banks in 1969—a large proportion of the rural poor continued to be outside the banking fold. A Working Group (Chairman: M. Narasimham) was set up in 1975 to explore the possibilities of evolving an alternative rural credit agency to benefit the rural poor. The Group recommended formation of a new set of regionally-oriented rural banks which would combine the local feel and familiarity of rural problems characteristic of cooperatives and the professionalism and large resource base of commercial banks. RRBs were set up as a sequel to this recommendation.

RRBs have a special place in the multi-agency approach adopted to provide agricultural and rural credit in India. These banks were established under the Regional Rural Banks Act, 1976 "with a view to developing the rural economy by providing, for the purpose of development of agriculture, trade, commerce, industry and other productive activities in the rural areas, credit and other facilities, particularly to small and marginal farmers, agricultural labourers, artisans and small entrepreneurs, and for matters connected therewith and incidental thereto".

The capital of RRBs is contributed by the Union Government, concerned State Government and a sponsor bank in the ratio 50:15:35. RRBs have played a key role in rural institutional financing in terms of geographical coverage, clientele outreach, business volume and contribution to the development of the rural economy.

Besides the RRBs, commercial and co-operative banks have been catering to the credit requirements of the rural sector. While the commercial banks, with their focus on profitability had certain limitations in accelerating agricultural credit, the cooperative banks efforts were also hampered by several financial weaknesses.

Though over the years the RRBs have been able to expand their outreach and business and meet the credit requirements of the poor, several weaknesses have emerged, eroding their profitability and viability. The recent focus of the Government of India on doubling the flow of credit to the agricultural sector has warranted a re-look at the relative roles of co-operative banks, RRBs and commercial banks.

As the very objective of setting up RRBs was to extend

adequate credit to the rural borrowers and particularly the economically weaker sections, owing to their rural orientation, there is a growing realization that RRBs could be used as an effective vehicle for credit delivery in the rural areas. There is, therefore, a need to devise ways and means to improve the health and viability of RRBs so as to reposition them in the credit delivery mechanism in India.

9.3 Amalgamation of RRBs

RRBs have been in sharp focus over the last few years with several measures initiated towards strengthening them and making them vibrant channels of credit delivery, particularly for the rural sector. The most prominent of these has been the process of state-wise amalgamation of RRBs sponsored by the same sponsor bank. As a result of the process of amalgamation, initiated in 2005, the number of RRBs in the country declined from 196 to 96 at the end of March 2007 and further to 56 at the end of March 2018. The Gross NPA ratio of RRBs stood at 9.1 percent for the year 2017-18.

The structural consolidation of RRBs has resulted in formation of new RRBs, which are financially stronger and bigger in size in terms of business volume and outreach. They will thus be able to take advantages of the economies of scale and reduce their operational costs. With the advantages of local feel and familiarity acquired by the RRBs, they would now be in a better position to achieve the objectives of rural development and financial inclusion.

9.4 Autonomy for RRBs

Further, measures have been taken to provide greater autonomy to RRBs and enlarge their business activities. A majority of the recommendations of the Task Force on Empowering RRB Boards for Operational Efficiency (Chairman: K.G. Karmakar) have already been implemented. RRBs have also been allowed to open currency chests, conduct

State government business as sub-agents of sponsor banks, take up corporate agency business without risk participation for distribution of all types of insurance products and open foreign currency non-resident (FCNR) accounts, subject to certain conditions. The branch licensing procedure for RRBs has been simplified with powers now delegated to the regional offices of Reserve Bank of India. The branch licensing policy has also been liberalised and the norms for opening new branches in hitherto uncovered districts have been relaxed. As a result, there has been a rapid increase in the number of branches of RRBs. The spread of RRBs has also increased and at the end of March 2018, they had a network of 21,747 branches.

9.5 RRBs as Vehicles of Financial Inclusion

RRBs have the potential to play a greater role in financial inclusion primarily because of their strategic geographical location in remote places in the country. In certain parts of the country, e.g. in the states of UP, Bihar and North-Eastern regions, the banking system mainly exists in the form of RRBs. Recognising the importance of achieving inclusive growth in the country, the RBI has permitted banks to utilise the services of non-governmental organizations (NGOs), self-help groups (SHGs), micro finance institutions (other than non-banking financial companies) and other civil society organisations as intermediaries to provide financial and banking services through the use of business facilitator and business correspondent (BC) models.

The BC model allows banks to do 'cash-in-cash-out' transactions at a location much closer to the rural population, thus addressing the last mile problem. However, customers in many parts of the country have to travel long distances, spend on transportation costs besides sacrificing their daily wages to visit the banks for doing their routine banking transactions and such inaccessibility contributes to the dormancy of many accounts in RRBs as well.

The objective of financial inclusion would be fully

achieved if RRBs are able to bring banking to the door step of the customers just as the commercial banks have started taking such initiatives. It is here that the large scale usage of information and communication technology (ICT) solutions lends support. RRB presence in rural areas leveraged by ICT would considerably enhance their reach, and delivery of banking services to the remote corners of the country.

The Committee on Financial Inclusion (Chairman: C. Rangarajan), also emphasised the role of IT and banking correspondents on a larger scale for achieving financial inclusion. The Committee envisaged that RRBs may extend services to unbanked areas and increase their credit to deposit ratio. The need for setting target for microfinance and financial inclusion was also envisaged. The Committee also recommended 100 percent financial inclusion of the large number of hitherto excluded farm households in order to reduce their indebtedness to the unregulated/informal sector.

The Committee estimated that 51.4 percent of the farm households do not get any credit from formal or informal sources. The North-Eastern Region, Eastern Region and Central Region taken together, account for 68 percent of the farm households having no access to credit.

The reach of RRBs particularly in regions and across population groups facing the brunt of financial exclusion is impressive. In rural areas, RRBs account for a substantial 37 percent of total offices of all scheduled commercial banks. In semi-urban areas, their share comes to 15 percent. With the process of merger strengthening, to some extent, the viability of the RRBs and also because of the local feel and familiarity they command, RRBs are in a unique position to play a very useful role in financial inclusion.

The RRBs need to be encouraged and supported in their financial inclusion initiatives for, *inter alia*, the following reasons:

1. Have presence in most of districts of the country.
2. Stronger presence in NER, ER and Central Regions.

3. Essential particularly for the areas where the financial exclusion rate is quite high.
4. Higher concentration of rural and semi-rural branches.
5. Have potential for intake of many more small accounts.
6. Though there are 56 RRBs with relatively reasonable performance, their net worth is not high and thus majority of RRBs are not financially very sound.

9.6 Factors Influencing the Performance of RRBs

Since their inception, the financial health of RRBs has been indifferent. A host of factors, both internal and external, have had a bearing on the performance of RRBs. Some of the major factors that had a bearing on the performance of RRBs are as follows:

9.6.1 Area of Operation and Clientele Base: The RRBs are constrained in their operations by their limited area of operation. This coupled with their narrow base of business activities and the low clientele base, has resulted in high risk exposure of RRBs. The customers of RRBs comprise small and marginal farmers, small-scale sector, small transport operators, SHGs, etc., whose credit requirements are mostly small. RRBs are unable to cross-subsidise their lending business as they do not generally provide credit to wealthy borrowers with large needs, thereby affecting their capacity to earn higher incomes.

There has been an uneven growth of RRBs due to the diffusion in the perceived objectives of RRBs over time. Despite the pressures of credit expansion, improvement in recovery performance, profit orientation and strict compliances to banking norms, the general perception has been that RRBs have got only social objectives, without any viability consideration, which has to be changed.

9.6.2 Capital Base and Organisational Structure: RRBs as a group have a low capital base, and their authorised capital of ₹ 1 crore places serious limitations on their business size. Furthermore, in the case of some of the RRBs their deposit liabilities are very large compared to their capital base. In view of their low capital base, in the event of inefficient use/misuse of funds resulting in a financial problem, the stakeholders would have to bail out the bank.

The size of financial assets, as well as linkages which are necessary for effective banking services has been limited by the small organizational structure of RRBs. This has also come in the way of growth in business volumes and garnering a larger share of the rural financial market.

9.6.3 Loan Delinquencies: RRBs loan recovery rates have declined over the years, resulting in a large over hang of NPAs which has come in their way of recycling funds and increasing the flow of credit to the rural sector. The directed lending policy for RRBs has resulted in low quality of assets. This coupled with high cost of funds and below cost interest rates on loans has led to high accumulated losses and piling up of bad assets in the case of many RRBs.

It is noteworthy that the target rural group has been one of the weaker and lowest strata of the Indian society. Smaller and marginal farmers and agricultural labourers always run short of money even for meeting their daily needs of life. Given the fact that most the villages in India still does not have clean drinking water and sanitation facilities, top it with lack of basic health facilities, makes them one of the most vulnerable groups in India. In any nature-made or man-made calamities, they are the most affected. Thus, credit facilities taken by the rural poor are mostly not utilized for specified productive objective for which it was made available.

For instance, when an agricultural labourer takes a small loan from an RRB for the purpose of buying a cow and small portion of it being only utilized for the stated purpose and the remaining amount used for household needs or for tending the sick. Such misappropriation seems very common and ultimately the labourer who took the loan would be unable to repay it. This naturally leads to substantial non-performing and lost assets in RRBs.

9.6.4 Cost Structure and Poor Financial Management Skills: RRBs are characterized by high cost of servicing numerous small accounts and high wage cost. Furthermore, RRBs get credit from sponsor banks and refinance from NABARD at rates of interest higher than the market rates. This places limitations on their ability to reduce the rates they charge to their ultimate borrowers, although they are compelled to do so on account of competition from banks.

Poor financial management skills, coupled with pressures from various quarters (like sponsor banks) appears to have resulted in inefficient allocation of resources by RRBs which in turn is reflected in the high incidence of NPAs and parking of large funds with sponsor banks.

9.6.5 Staff Structure: Limited exposure and lack of appropriate training, has resulted in RRBs staff lacking the necessary skills and capacity to cater to the changing requirements of the rural sector. Furthermore, the ban on recruitment has also resulted in ageing staff structure constraining efficiency in operations. Uniform norms and personnel policies have been applied to RRBs through out the country ignoring local touch thereby causing staff unrest, poor industrial relations, innumerable litigations and lowering of staff morale as also their involvement with the development tasks.

The chairmen of most of the RRBs are from sponsor banks, which limits the freedom and decision making capacity of the RRBs. Even for small matters, RRBs have to refer to their sponsor banks, which leads to delay in decision-making and reduces efficiency. Furthermore, the board of directors of RRBs may not always function effectively as some of the members do not have necessary skills and expertise to take important financial decisions.

9.6.6 Dependence on Sponsor Banks: Another weakness observed in the case of RRBs is their failure to adequately integrate with the financial markets of the country due to their heavy dependence on sponsor banks for financial/business initiatives. RRBs are also some times perceived as potential competitors, due to the presence of the sponsor banks in the same area of operation. Despite the best intentions at the policy levels in sponsor banks, the RRBs have suffered at the ground level wherever there has been any conflict of business interests of RRBs and their sponsor banks. RRBs have therefore, not been able to establish systems and procedures required for providing efficient services to their clients, as also for efficient management of their financial resources.

Besides the above, functioning of RRBs has also been affected by certain legacy problems and policy constraints. The administered interest rate regime prevalent in the system for a considerably long time influenced the performance of RRBs. These banks were required to lend at low interest rates as they were financing the weaker sections and at the same time allowed to pay a slightly higher rate of interest on deposits.

The RRBs were required to maintain their local character or flavour with a view to identifying more with the rural populace. This was initially embedded in the wage structure designed for these banks. However, the change in the wage structure of RRBs by bringing them on par with the commercial banks led to higher wage costs, thereby affecting the performance of these banks.

9.7 Restructuring of RRBs

In order to reposition RRBs as an effective instrument of credit delivery in the Indian financial system, an Internal Working Group on RRBs (Chairman: A.V. Sardesai) was set up by the RBI in February 2005 to examine various alternatives available within the existing legal framework for strengthening the RRBs and making them viable rural financial institutions. The Group, in its final report submitted in June 2005, made several recommendations for restructuring the RRBs. The main recommendations of the Working Group related to restructuring options, change of sponsor banks, minimum capital requirements, governance and management, regulation and supervision.

The major recommendations of the Group were as follows:

1. To improve the operational viability of RRBs, the route of merger/amalgamation of RRBs may be considered along two lines: (a) merger between RRBs of the same sponsor bank in the same State, and (b) merger of RRBs sponsored by different banks in the same State.
2. A change in sponsor banks may, in some cases, help improve competitiveness, work culture and efficiency of concerned RRBs for which new banks, both public and private sector, could be considered.
3. Merged entities and existing RRBs that have accumulated losses can be capitalised to wipe out the losses and satisfy minimum capital requirement. The CRAR may initially be kept at 5 percent.
4. For those RRBs which may not turn around within a specified time limit, say 3 to 5 years, an exit route may be considered subject to extant legal provisions.
5. Process of appointment of Chairmen of RRBs may be re-examined to explore the possibility of appointing them from the open market through a transparent process.
6. Boards of RRBs may be strengthened by making them broad-based through inclusion of professionals such as agricultural experts, bankers etc.
7. An appropriate recruitment policy, providing for greater flexibility and freedom, may be required for RRBs.
8. An appropriate incentive structure, career planning, relevant training, especially in skill upgradation and information technology, be evolved for employees of RRBs.
9. It would be appropriate if both the regulatory and supervisory functions relating to RRBs are exercised by the RBI.
10. RRBs may be encouraged to actively consider distribution of products of mutual fund/insurance companies, rationalisation of branch network, participate in consortium lending within their areas of operations.
11. RRBs may be considered for currency chest facility and empowered to collect taxes by the State Governments.

9.8 Manpower Challenges of RRBs

Measures have also been taken to address the manpower challenges in the RRBs. It is known that RRBs do not have their own training establishments so far. The existing training facilities available for RRB staff are Bankers Institute for Rural Development, Lucknow, College of Agricultural Banking, Pune, regional training colleges of NABARD at Mangalore and Bolpur, and the sponsor bank training institutes. However, all these institutions (other than sponsor bank training institutes) provide training only to officers and not to clerical or subordinate staff.

The Committee to Formulate a Comprehensive Human Resource Policy for RRBs (Chairman: Y.S.P. Thorat), had, in its report recommended that RRBs should have an exclusive training cell within the personnel department at head office and bestow more attention to the training function. It also recommended that sponsor banks can consider earmarking in any one training institute in a state, at least one channel to cater to the training requirements of all RRBs within the state and/or the adjoining states.

9.9 Computerisation in RRBs

The need for computerisation in RRBs had been felt since long and some RRBs had been taking some steps in that direction. In July 2001, Government of India and NABARD advised the RRBs to initiate immediate steps so that head office, area office and a minimum of 50 percent of the branches were computerised in a phased manner in the next 5 years. Sponsor banks were also advised to formulate RRB-wise Action Plans, keeping in view the financial position of RRBs, infrastructure facilities available in their command area and the business potential of the RRB branches. Necessary support to implement the programme was also required to come from the sponsor bank.

NABARD made a beginning by extending support to select RRBs by providing PCs, peripherals, standard software packages as also customised MIS package and training inputs under its Swiss Agency for Development and Cooperation (SDC) programme. A review made by NABARD in respect of 152 RRBs in 2005 indicated that only 9 banks had reported achieving 100 percent computerisation. Most of the RRBs were lagging behind the target of computerising 50 percent of their branches. The Task Force on Empowering RRBs for Operational Efficiency (Chairman: K.G. Karmakar) had made the following observations regarding the computerisation scenario in RRBs:

1. Level of computerisation is far behind schedule.
2. Even RRBs of same sponsor banks although following the same technology, are at different levels of computerisation due to varied financial health, environment, local conditions which has become a problem when such RRBs have been amalgamated.
3. Computerisation needs both capital and recurring expenses which are beyond the capability of some of the banks.
4. RRBs, which have progressed well, have adopted a particular technology mainly of the sponsor bank and invested sizeable amounts.
5. A few RRBs reaped the benefit of hosting their own website by way of mobilisation of deposits from non traditional segments.
6. A few of them established direct links with money market operators for investments.
7. Internet facilities have been used for faster communication with techno savvy customers and other agencies.

These observations highlighted the varying status of RRBs with regard to computerisation.

The status of computerisation at the end of March 2007 as reported by 76 of the 96 RRBs to the Committee to Formulate a Comprehensive Human Resource Policy for RRBs (Chairman: Y.S.P. Thorat) indicated that 35 of the reporting banks had achieved 100 percent computerisation while 25 banks had achieved 50 to 100 percent computerisation.

9.9.1 Working Group on Technology Upgradation of Regional Rural Banks, August 2008: In RBI's Mid-term Review of Annual Policy for 2007-08, it was stated that in order to prepare RRBs to adopt appropriate technology and migrate to core banking solutions (CBS) for better customer services, it was proposed to constitute a Working Group with representatives from RBI, NABARD, sponsor banks and RRBs for preparing a road-map for migration to core banking solutions by RRBs.

Accordingly, a Working Group (Chairman: G. Srinivasan) was set up with the following terms of reference:

1. To determine the nature of core banking solutions required for RRBs having regard to the range of their business and customer service.
2. To examine various options including extending core banking solutions of the sponsor banks to their RRBs with necessary modifications and firewalls.
3. To estimate the likely costs involved and funding and training arrangements that may be necessary.
4. To draw out a time-bound road map for implementation.

The Working Group was also requested to examine the possibility of using solar power generating devices for meeting the power requirements of RRBs, especially in remote areas.

The Working Group was of the opinion that RRBs cannot afford to remain isolated from the technological developments sweeping the banking sector. With the commercial banks racing towards a higher degree of technological sophistication, the RRBs would be required to adopt technology for improving the quality of their customer service. However, given the different levels at which the different RRBs are presently placed in regard to their status of computerisation, a "one strategy fits all" approach may not be workable.

The Working Group was of the view that as a matter of policy, all RRBs should begin moving towards CBS. The CBS in RRBs should be geared towards better management control and monitoring, wider range of services offered and enhanced level of customer satisfaction. Adoption of CBS would lead to uniformity in work environment, more informed decision-making, centralised processing and better MIS and reporting and improved regulatory compliance.

The Working Group also examined the use of solar power devices such as solar photovoltaic cells for RRBs, particularly in respect of branches located in remote areas which are not assured of continuous power supply. In this context, the experience of one of the RRBs in Uttar Pradesh, which has made a beginning in this direction, was also studied.

10

Digital Technology in Banking Sector

Financial sector, especially the banking sector, has been a major beneficiary from the inroads made by IT. Many new processes, products and services offered by banks and other financial intermediaries are now IT-centred. Banks have traditionally been in the forefront of harnessing technology to improve their products, services and efficiency. They have, over a long time, been using electronic and telecommunication networks for delivering a wide range of value added products and services. The delivery channels include, inter alia, direct dial-up connections, private networks, public networks and the devices including telephone, personal computers (PCs), automated teller machines (ATMs), networking of ATMs in the form of shared payment networks, and core banking solutions.

With the popularity of PCs, easy access to internet and world wide web (www), internet is increasingly used by banks as a channel for receiving instructions and delivering their products and services to their customers. This form of banking is generally referred to as internet banking, although the range of products and services offered by different banks vary widely both in their content and sophistication.

10.1 Internet Banking

10.1.1 Internet Banking and Electronic Banking: Electronic banking (e-banking) is a generic term encompassing internet banking, telephone banking, mobile banking etc. In other words, it is a process of delivery of banking services and products through electronic channels such as satellite, telephone, internet, cell phone etc. The concept and scope of e-banking is still evolving. Internet banking is a major component of e-banking.

Internet banking offers different online services like balance enquiry, requests for cheque books, recording stop-payment instructions, balance transfer instructions, account opening and other forms of traditional banking services. These are mostly traditional services offered through internet as a new delivery channel. Banks are also offering payment services on behalf of their customers who shop in different e-shops, e-malls etc.

10.1.2 Levels of Banking Services Offered through Internet: Internet banking applications run on diverse platforms and operating systems and use different architectures. The product may support centralized (bank-wide) operations or branch level automation. It may have a distributed, client server or three-tier architecture based on a file system. Moreover, the product may run on computer systems of various types ranging from PCs, open (Unix based) systems, to proprietary main frames. These products allow different levels of access to the customers and different range of facilities. The products accessible through Internet can be classified into three types based on the levels of access granted.

- **Basic Level Services (or Information Only Systems):** These refer to websites of banks which disseminate information on different products and services offered to customers and members of public in general. A bank may receive and reply to queries of customers through email. General purpose information like interest rates, branch locations, product features, loan and deposit calculators are provided on the web (www) site of a bank. The sites also allow downloading of application forms. Interactivity is limited to a simple form of email. No identification or authentication of customers is done and there is no interaction between the bank's production system (where current data of accounts are kept and transactions are processed) and the customer.
- **Simple Transactional Systems:** These allow customers to

submit their instructions, applications for different services, queries on their account balances etc., but do not permit any fund-based transactions on their accounts. These systems provide customer-specific information in the form of account balances, transaction details, statement of account etc. The information is still largely *read only*. Identification and authentication of customer takes place using relatively simple techniques (like passwords). Information is fetched from the production system of the bank in either the batch mode or offline. Thus, the main application system of the bank is not directly accessed.

- **Fully Transactional Websites:** These allow the customers to operate on their accounts for transfer of funds, payment of different bills, subscribing to other products of the bank and to transact purchase and sale of securities etc. These systems provide bi-directional transaction capabilities. The bank allows customers to submit transactions on its systems and these directly update customers' accounts. Therefore, security and control system need to be strongest here.

The above forms of internet banking services are offered by traditional banks as an additional method of serving the customer or by new banks who deliver banking services primarily through internet or other electronic delivery channels as the value added services. Some of these banks are known as *virtual banks* or *internet-only-banks* (IOBs) and may not have any physical presence in a country despite offering different banking services. Thus, internet banking is nothing more than traditional banking services delivered through an electronic communication backbone, viz. internet. However, in the process it has thrown open issues which have ramifications beyond what a new delivery channel would normally envisage. Hence, it has compelled regulators world over to take note of this emerging channel.

10.1.3 Internet Banking in India: Internet banking—both as a medium of delivery of banking services and as a strategic tool for business development—has gained wide acceptance internationally and is fast catching up in India with more and more banks entering the fray. India can be said to be on the threshold of a major banking revolution with net banking having already been unveiled.

The growth potential of internet banking in India is immense. Further incentives provided by banks would dissuade customers from visiting physical branches, and thus get 'hooked' to the convenience of arm-chair banking. The facility of accessing their accounts from anywhere in the world by using a home computer with internet connection, is particularly fascinating to non-resident Indians and high net worth individuals having multiple bank accounts.

Costs of banking service through the internet form a fraction of costs through conventional methods. The cost conscious banks in the country have therefore actively considered use of internet as a channel for providing services. Fully computerized banks, with better management of their customer base are in a stronger position to cross-sell their products through this channel.

A. Products and Services Offered: Banks in India are at different stages of the web-enabled banking cycle. Initially, a bank, which is not having a website, allows its customer to communicate with it through an email address; communication is limited to a small number of branches and offices which have access to this email account. As yet, many scheduled commercial banks in India are still in the first stage of internet banking operations.

With gradual adoption of information technology, the bank puts up a website that provides general information on the banks, its location, services available e.g. loan and deposits products, application forms for downloading and email option for enquiries and feedback. It is largely a marketing or advertising tool. Customers are required to fill in applications on the internet and can later receive loans or other products requested for at their local branch. A few banks provide the customer to enquire into his demat account (securities/shares) holding details, transaction details and status of instructions given by him.

Some of the banks permit customers to interact with them and transact electronically with them. Such services include request for opening of accounts, requisition for cheque books, stop payment of cheques, viewing and printing statements of accounts, movement of funds between accounts within the same bank, querying on status of requests, instructions for opening of letters of credit and bank guarantees etc.

Banks are thus looking to position themselves as one-stop financial shops. Some banks have tied up with computer training companies, computer manufacturers, internet services providers and portals for expanding their internet banking services, and widening their customer base. Setting up of internet kiosks and permeation through the cable television route to widen customer base are other priority areas in the agendas of the more aggressive players.

Banks providing internet banking services have been entering into agreements with their customers setting out the terms and conditions of the services. The terms and conditions include information on the access through user-id and secret password minimum balance and charges, authority to the bank for carrying out transactions performed through the service, liability of the user and the bank, disclosure of personal information for statistical analysis and credit scoring also, non-transferability of the facility, notices and termination etc.

The race for market supremacy is compelling banks in India to adopt the latest technology on the internet in a bid to capture new markets and customers. Under mobile banking services, customers can scan their accounts to seek balance and payments status or instruct banks to issue cheques, pay bills or deliver statements of accounts.

Compared to banks abroad, Indian banks offering online services still have a long way to go. For online banking to reach a critical mass, there has to be sufficient number of users and the sufficient infrastructure in place. Though various security options like line encryption, branch connection encryption, firewalls, digital certificates, automatic sign-offs, random pop-ups and disaster recovery sites are in place or are being looked at, there is as yet no certification authority in India offering public key infrastructure which is absolutely necessary for online banking. The customer can only be assured of a secured conduit for its online activities if an authority certifying digital signatures is in place. The communication bandwidth presently available in India is also not enough to meet the needs of high priority services like online banking and trading. Banks offering online facilities need to have an effective disaster recovery plan along with comprehensive risk management measures. Banks offering online facilities also need to calculate their downtime losses, because even a few minutes of downtime in a week could mean substantial losses.

Some banks even today do not have uninterrupted power supply unit or systems to take care of prolonged power breakdown. Proper encryption of data and effective use of passwords are also matters that leave a lot to be desired. Systems and processes have to be put in place to ensure that errors do not take place.

Users of internet banking services are required to fill up the application forms online and send a copy of the same by mail or fax to the bank. A contractual agreement is entered into by the customer with the bank for using the internet banking services. In this way, personal data in the applications forms is being held by the bank providing the service. The contract details are often one-sided, with the bank having the absolute discretion to amend or supplement any of the terms at any time. For these reasons domestic customers for whom other access points such as ATMs, telebanking, personal contact etc. are available, are often hesitant to use the internet banking services offered by Indian banks.

Internet banking, as an additional delivery channel, may, therefore, be attractive/appealing as a value added service to domestic customers. Non-resident Indians for whom it is expensive and time consuming to access their bank accounts maintained in India find net banking very convenient and useful.

B. Role of the Reserve Bank of India: The RBI has played a proactive role in the implementation of IT in the banking sector. IT-based initiatives are focused on meeting the three-pronged objective of better house keeping, improved customer service and overall efficiency. The RBI has come out with a Financial Sector Technology Vision Document outlining the approach to be followed for IT implementation for the medium-term period of about three years.

Several initiatives taken by the Government of India as well as the Reserve Bank of India (RBI) have facilitated the development of internet banking in India. As a regulator and supervisor, the RBI has made considerable progress in consolidating the existing payment and settlement systems, and in upgrading technology with a view to establishing an efficient, integrated and secure system functioning in a real time environment, which has further helped the development of internet banking in India. The Government of India enacted the Information Technology Act, 2000 with effect from October 17, 2000, which provides legal recognition to electronic transactions and other means of electronic commerce.

The RBI has been gearing up to upgrading itself as a regulator and supervisor of the technologically dominated financial system. It issued guidelines on Risks and Control in Computer and Telecommunication System in February 1998 to all the banks advising them to evaluate the risks inherent in the systems and put in place adequate control mechanisms to address these risks, which can be broadly put under three heads, *viz.*, IT environment risks, IT operations risks and product risks.

The existing regulatory framework over banks has also

been extended to internet banking. These guidelines cover various issues that would fall within the framework of technology, security standards and legal and regulatory issues. Virtual banks, which have no offices and function only online are not permitted to offer electronic banking services in India and that only banks licensed under the Banking Regulation Act and having a physical presence in India are allowed to offer such services. Further, banks are required to report to the RBI every breach or failure of security systems and procedures in internet banking, while the RBI at its discretion may decide to commission special audit/inspection of such banks.

As per guidelines, banks no longer need any prior approval of the Reserve Bank for offering the internet banking services. Nevertheless, banks must have their internet policy and they need to ensure that it is in line with parameters as set by it.

RBI has taken the initiative for facilitating real time funds transfer through the real time gross settlement (RTGS) system. Under the RTGS system, transmission, processing and settlements of the instructions will be done on a continuous basis. Gross settlement in a real time mode eliminates credit and liquidity risks. Any member of the system will be able to access it through only one specified gateway in order to ensure rigorous access control measures at the user level. Further, generic architecture, both domestic and cross border, aimed at providing inter-connectivity across banks has been accepted for implementation by RBI.

C. Challenges: Innovations are mixed blessings. They bring benefits as well as pose challenges. Innovations in information technology (IT) are no exception to this rule. The most prominent challenge arising from these innovations relates to the concept of security. Considering the scope for fraud in the electronic banking area and the possibility of contagion, the Reserve Bank of India—as a regulator and supervisor—has been proactive in addressing the risks associated with electronic banking. The RBI has been promptly addressing issues related to fraud with the use of electronic banking facility. Even after issuing guidelines for a secured electronic banking, the RBI advises the banks, from time to time, on control mechanisms to combat such frauds.

In India, the legal infrastructure for promoting internet banking has not yet been put in place in a comprehensive manner. India does not have a licensed certifying authority appointed by the Controller of Certifying Authorities to issue digital signature certificates. Also, India is not yet a signatory to the International Cyber Crime Treaty, which seeks to intensify co-operation among different signatory nations for exchanging information concerning crime and cyber criminals. Further, there are unresolved legislative issues related to cyber crime laws, clarification relating to regulatory authority over e-money products, consumer protection and privacy laws. To make the electronic banking operations in India more widespread, secure and efficient, these issues need to be addressed by relevant authorities.

As the banking practices and legislations concerning electronic banking are still in the process of evolution in India and abroad because of technological innovations, there is a need for a constant review of various legislations and regulatory framework relating to banking and commerce. The RBI is monitoring and reviewing the legal and other requirements of electronic banking on a continuous basis to ensure that the e-banking would develop on sound lines and the e-banking related challenges would not pose a threat to financial stability.

10.2 Mobile Banking

10.2.1 Introduction: Developments in mobile telephony, as also the mobile phone density in the India, present a unique opportunity to leverage the mobile platform to meet the objectives and challenges of financial inclusion. By harnessing the potential of mobile technology, large sections of the un-banked and under-banked society can be empowered to become inclusive through the use of electronic banking services.

The Payment and Settlement Systems (PSS) Act, 2007 empowers the Reserve Bank of India to authorize and regulate entities operating payment systems in the country. RBI has, over a period of time, placed importance on the move towards electronic payments and thereby a *less-cash* society. Towards this end, the RBI has been promoting and nurturing the growth of various modes of electronic payments including the pre-paid payment instruments, card payments, mobile banking etc.

RBI's Vision Document 2019-21 on Payment and Settlement Systems, released on May 15, 2019, has the core theme of Empowering Exceptional (E) Payment Experience

The Vision 2021 for payment and settlement systems in India enhances the strong foundation built over the last two decades. While the pursuit towards a *less cash* society continues, accompanied by the ambition to have a less-card India as well, the endeavour is to also ensure increased efficiency, uninterrupted availability of safe, secure, accessible and affordable payment systems as also to serve segments of the population which are hitherto untouched by the payment systems.

10.2.2 Mobile Banking: Regulatory Framework: Recognising the potential of mobile as a channel for offering financial services in the country, RBI issued the first set of guidelines on mobile banking in October 2008. The mandate was that all transactions should originate from one bank account and terminate in another bank account. At this time, a few banks had already started offering information-based services like balance enquiry, stop payment instruction of cheques, transactions enquiry, location of the nearest ATM/branch etc. through this medium.

The guidelines issued by RBI in October 2008, permitted banks to facilitate funds transfer from one bank account to another bank account, both for personal remittances and purchase of goods and services. Banks were directed on the regulatory/supervisory issues, registration of customers for mobile banking, to ensure technology standards, interoperability, inter-bank clearing and settlement arrangements for fund transfers, customer grievance and redressal mechanism and transaction limits in an attempt to ensure safe, secure transfer of funds.

Under extant regulatory prescriptions, there is no monetary restriction on fund transfer effected through mobile banking as it is left to the risk perception of each bank and policies approved by their respective Boards. However, end-to-end encryption for transactions in excess of ₹ 5,000 has been mandated by RBI. Similarly, mobile as a channel for funds transfer from a bank account for cash payout to a beneficiary who does not have a bank account at ATMs/BCs—₹ 10,000 per transaction with a cap of ₹ 25,000 per beneficiary has also been permitted by RBI (under the Domestic Money Transfer Guidelines).

In line with these guidelines, banks have been offering mobile banking services to their customers through various channels such as SMS, USSD channel, mobile banking application etc. However, real time inter-bank mobile banking payments have been facilitated through the setting up of the inter-bank mobile payment services (IMPS), now termed as immediate payment service, and operated by the NPCI with the approval of RBI. The IMPS has enhanced the efficiency of mobile banking by enabling real time transfer of funds between bank accounts and providing a centralised inter-bank settlement service for mobile banking transactions. The IMPS has also been enhanced to support merchant payments using mobile phones to promote less cash society.

As per RBI's Annual Report 2017-18, mobile banking services witnessed a growth of 92 percent in volume terms. The number of registered customers rose by 54 percent and stood at 251 million at end-March 2018 up from 163 million at end-March 2017.

10.2.3 Various Channels for Mobile Banking:

A. Mobile Banking: SMS-based Channel: SMS is a popular and widely used channel in mobile phones. It is ubiquitously available in all handsets irrespective of make and model and also GSM and CDMA enabled handsets. Most customers are very conversant with the SMS channel and use the same for various services including the short messaging. Many popular mobile VAS services such as cricket, jokes, horoscopes, etc. are based on SMS and used widely by customers.

Given the advantages offered by SMS channel, many banks have offered mobile banking services through the SMS channel. This includes non-financial services such as balance enquiry, mini statement, cheque book request, transaction alerts etc., and financial services such as funds transfer, mobile/DTH recharge, bill payments etc.

B. Mobile Banking: USSD-based Channel: Unstructured supplementary service data (USSD) is a protocol used by GSM cellular telephones to communicate with the telecom service provider's systems. USSD can be used for WAP browsing, pre-paid call-back service, mobile-money services, location-based content services, menu-based information services, and as part of configuring the phone on the network.

USSD messages are up to 182 alphanumeric characters in length. Unlike short message service (SMS) messages, USSD messages create a real-time connection during a USSD session. The connection remains open, allowing a two-way exchange of a sequence of data. This makes USSD more interactive and advantageous than services that use SMS.

USSD platform which is MNO dependent can be efficiently used by the mobile banking platforms. Realizing the benefits and potential of USSD-based mobile banking, some of the banks have launched USSD-based mobile banking services, e.g. State Bank of India, Canara Bank, ICICI Bank, with the help of telecom aggregators who in turn have tied up with few MNOs. For instance, ICICI Bank has tied up with Idea, Aircel, Tata Docomo, Reliance and MTNL for offering USSD platform to its customers on their GSM network.

C. Mobile Banking: Application-based: All banks who have received the approval from RBI for mobile banking are offering the application-based mobile banking channel to their customers. Customers can download the mobile banking application and perform variety of services including the following: (a) non-financial transactions such as balance enquiry, mini statement, cheque book request, (b) financial transactions such as funds transfer, mobile/DTH recharge, bill payments etc

The mobile application is offered on various platforms such as Java, Symbian, Blackberry OS, Windows, Android, Apple iOS etc. Many Banks have made the mobile application available in the app stores such as Google, Apple, Blackberry, etc. for easy search and download by the customers.

Following are the advantages of the application-based mobile banking:

- Applications once downloaded are easy to use for the customers who are proficient in using the smart phone based applications.
- Banks have made these applications compliant with most of the latest operating systems covering the large range of smart phones in use.
- It has been experienced by the banks that once customer has used the application-based mobile banking, he continues to use the same unless there is a change of the handset and/or mobile number.
- The application-based mobile banking can also communicate using SMS and GPRS (data) channels with the mobile banking system of the bank.

10.2.4 Challenges Faced by Banks in Providing Mobile Banking Services: Despite the potential for mobile banking and the regulatory provisions enabling greater use of mobiles as a channel for financial services in general, and for financial inclusion in particular, banks are facing some challenges in taking mobile banking to the desired level. These challenges are essentially in two fronts:

1. Customer enrolment related issues.
2. Technical issues.

A. Customer Enrolment Related Issues: These are as under:

1. Mobile number registration.
2. M-PIN generation process.
3. Concerns relating to security are a factor affecting on-boarding of customers.
4. Bank staff education.
5. Customer education.

(a) Mobile Number Registration: For a customer, in order to conduct a mobile payment transaction, his/her mobile number needs to be registered with the bank. The process for mobile number registration is implemented differently across banks. Currently, the process for mobile number registration involves the following:

- Customer mandatorily needs to go to the bank branch for most of the banks to register his number and fill in the application form (paper-based). After verification, his number gets registered in the CBS and in the bank's mobile banking system.
- Some leading banks have provided the facility for customer to register mobile number at their bank's ATMs using 2FA authentication of ATM card + ATM PIN.

In both the above cases, the customer needs to physically go to the branch/ATM in order to register their mobile number, which acts as a barrier in many cases, besides delaying the entire process. Further, even where the above process of registration through ATMs is provided, it is restricted to the use of own-bank ATMs and the same is not possible at present by going to any other bank ATMs. The process for mobile number registration needs to be simpler for customer to get on-boarded.

(b) M-PIN Generation: M-PIN is the second factor of authentication that customer needs to use in order to conduct mobile banking transaction. Customer needs M-PIN from his respective bank in order to get started with mobile payments. Currently, the process for M-PIN generation is implemented differently across banks, and involves the following:

- For most banks, after the mobile number registration at branch/any bank ATM, customer receives M-PIN via SMS on their registered mobile number. In certain cases, customer receives the M-PIN through postal mail.
- Some leading banks have provided the facility for generating and changing M-PIN from the handset itself using the mobile banking application and providing the authentication parameters as required by the bank (e.g. debit card details such as debit card number, ATM PIN, expiry date). These inputs are captured and sent through registered mobile number, for the purpose of M-PIN generation.
- Some leading banks have also provided the facility to generate and change M-PIN through alternate channels such as IVR, ATM, and internet banking. Customer may be able to make merchant payment using just his mobile number and M-PIN/OTP on the merchant interface. The M-pin can be only interfaced on acquiring bank's interface such as USSD, Application etc. for security reasons. The merchant based interfaces can accept OTP (one-time password) for authentication.

(c) Concerns Related to Security: One of the major factors affecting customer on-boarding and usage of mobile banking services is the concern relating to security of transactions effected using the mobile phone. While mobile banking application is an end-to-end encrypted channel, the other access channels viz. SMS, USSD, IVR, are not end-to-end encrypted. However, in order to enjoy the higher level of security available in the application-based mobile banking, the customer's handset has to be GPRS-enabled.

Since SMS facility is available on all handsets, the issue of security can be addressed if the SMS can be encrypted end-to-end, thus allaying any concerns relating to lack of security in this channel.

In addition to this, another important aspect adding to the

concerns on the part of customers relate to how their complaints and grievances will be addressed for transacting on this channel—whether through their bank or through their mobile service provider.

(d) Bank Staff Training: For effective and efficient implementation of providing mobile banking facilities to the customers it is imperative that the banks staff is well versed and thoroughly trained in various aspects of the mobile banking.

(e) Customer Education: Banks must continue to invest in handholding and educating customers to increase the awareness of various aspects of mobile banking. Banks collectively may invest in marketing and advertising for widespread promotion of mobile banking.

B. Technical Issues: Technical aspects which are posing a challenge relate to the following:

1. Access channels for transactions.
2. Cumbersome transaction process.
3. Co-ordination with MNOs in mobile banking eco-system.

(a) Access Channels for Transaction: Once the customer mobile number is registered and M-PIN is generated, customer may use any of the access channels provided by the bank for conducting mobile banking transactions. Currently, while most banks have provided mobile banking application and SMS facility as access channels, a few banks have also provided other access channels such as USSD, WAP, IVR, etc. Some banks also provide a combination of a few of these channels (application + SMS, application + USSD) for offering better security.

(b) Cumbersome Transaction Process: In the present scenario, with various banks offering various channels for their customers to undertake mobile banking transactions, the user experience is certainly not uniform across banks/channels. The customer is required to provide different set of inputs (authentication parameters) for each type of access channel, thus making the entire transaction process cumbersome.

(c) Co-ordination with MNOs in Mobile Banking Eco-system: In order to offer a more secure and better user experience to their customers through their mobile banking channels, banks need a greater level of coordination with the telecom service providers.

10.2.5 RBI's Technical Committee on Mobile Banking, 2014: Reserve Bank of India constituted a Technical Committee (Chairman: B. Sambamurthy), to study in depth, the present challenges faced in mobile banking, the adoption of particular technologies to meet the requirements of banks as well as vast numbers of mobile users and draw up a road-map for implementation of the solutions. [1]

Major recommendations of the Committee were as under:

1. Banks need to explore other means of facilitating customer/user registration process for mobile banking which does not require a visit to the bank branch. The potential of inter-operable ATM networks and business correspondent arrangements has to be effectively harnessed towards meeting this objective. Standardization is required in: (a) user registration for mobile banking, (b) user authentication process and (c) user interfaces. Recognising the crucial role that customer/user awareness plays in adoption of any technology for financial transactions, as well as the need for optimal utilization of resources, the joint customer education programmes by banks will go a long way in facilitating usage of mobile banking.
2. Mobile network operators (MNOs) need to see a business model in it for themselves and play out their role in ensuring mobile banking reaches its full potential by co-operating with banks in their endeavour to provide the appropriate technology/channel to the targeted users. Mobile banking can result in customer stickiness and reduce churn for MNOs. Mobile banking can increase revenue to MNOs and reduce costs to banks. The current solutions already provided by banks and various

technological alternatives available can be put in place through a concerted effort between banks and telecom service providers.

3. Common mobile banking applications and common technological platforms need to be built for reaping the benefits of *network effects*. While bank-specific applications and individual platforms have a major role in building brand loyalty, an alternate uniform/common platform, interoperability and similar seamless transactional experience to the users/customers of all banks would encourage mobile banking.
4. The Government of India can explore the options of offering fiscal incentives/economic subventions to the stakeholders in order to ensure participation of various players to offer the solutions recommended here in this Report. The committee would like to draw attention to similar law *Lei Do Bem* (Law of the Goods) enacted by Brazil in October 2013 which mandates that smart phones give visibility to Brazilian made apps by either pre-loading phones with these home-grown apps or providing a dedicated marketplace on smart phones to display them. Similar intervention in India can support and incentivise the relevant stakeholders to either *pre-burn* common mobile banking application on mobile handsets/SIM cards or send *over-the-air* using dynamic STK to facilitate financial transactions. This is a *build-it-they-will-come* approach.

Endnote

1. Reserve Bank of India, *Report of the Technical Committee on Mobile Banking*, January 2014.

Part III
Financial Markets Evolution and Reforms

11

Financial Markets: An Introduction

Financial markets in India have seen considerable development since financial sector reforms were initiated in the 1990s. Given the imperatives of the prevailing context, the initial nudge had to be provided through specific policy instruments and actions, but over a period of time these markets have acquired a dynamic of their own. The process of transition in respect of all financial market segments has been largely disruption-free, accommodating the unique features of the existing system while trying to align with the best international practices.

11.1 Importance of Financial Markets

A well-functioning financial market enables efficient use of market-based instruments of monetary policy by improving interest rate signals in the economy. Apart from enhancing the efficiency of monetary policy, deep and well-functioning financial markets promote mobilisation of domestic savings and improve the allocative efficiency of financial intermediation, and foster the necessary conditions to emerge as an international or a regional financial centre. Strong domestic financial markets also act as a buffer against external disturbances and help in absorbing shocks to the domestic banking system during crises. Further, they provide incentives for development of hedging instruments, and lower macroeconomic volatility and financial instability. Efficient financial markets also have several indirect benefits such as rapid accumulation of physical and human capital, more stable investment financing, and faster technological progress.

Developed and well-integrated financial markets are critical for sustaining high growth, for the effective conduct of monetary policy, for developing a diversified financial system, financial integration and ensuring financial stability. The question therefore is not whether developed financial markets are needed, but how to go about in developing them fully. Financial markets presently deal with complex and sophisticated products. Introduction of such products would require clear regulatory frameworks, appropriate institutions and development of human resource skills. The speed for further changes in the financial markets would thus depend on how quickly are we able to meet these requirements.

The need for developed financial markets also arises in the context of increasing integration of domestic financial markets with international financial markets. The concept of globalisation is no longer restricted to its traditional sense—variety of cross-border transactions in goods and services—but also extends to international capital flows, driven by rapid and widespread diffusion of technology. In fact, most of the literature in recent years on globalisation has centred around financial integration due to the emergence of worldwide financial markets and the possibility of better access to external financing for a variety of domestic entities.

Financial market development is a complex and time-consuming process. There are no short cuts for developing well-functioning markets with depth and liquidity. Some of the preconditions for financial market reform are the following.

1. Macroeconomic stability.
2. Sound and efficient financial institutions and structure.
3. Prudential regulation and supervision.
4. Strong creditor rights.
5. Contract enforcement.

11.2 Types of Financial Markets

The financial markets can broadly be divided into money and capital market.

11.2.1 Money Market: Money market is a market for debt securities that pay off in the short term usually less than one year, for example the market for 90-days treasury bills. This market encompasses the trading and issuance of short term non equity debt instruments including treasury bills, commercial papers, bankers acceptance, certificates of deposits etc.

11.2.2 Capital Market: Capital market is a market for long-term debt and equity shares. In this market, the capital funds comprising of both equity and debt are issued and traded. This also includes private placement sources of debt and equity as well as organized markets like stock exchanges. Capital market can be further divided into primary and secondary markets.

In the primary market securities are offered to public for subscription for the purpose of raising capital or fund. Secondary market is an equity trading venue in which already existing/pre-issued securities are traded among investors.

Secondary market refers to a market where securities are traded after being initially offered to the public in the primary market and/or listed on the stock exchange. Majority of the trading is done in the secondary market. Secondary market comprises of equity markets and the debt markets.

For the general investor, the secondary market provides an efficient platform for trading of his securities. For the management of the company, secondary equity markets serve as a monitoring and control conduit by facilitating value-enhancing control activities, enabling implementation of incentive-based management contracts, and aggregating information (via price discovery) that guides management decisions.

11.3 Regulation/Supervision of Financial Markets in India

Financial markets in India have evidenced significant development since the financial sector reforms initiated in the 1990s. The development of these markets has been done in a calibrated, sequenced manner and in step with those in other markets in the real economy. The emphasis has been on strengthening price discovery, easing restrictions on flows or transactions, lowering transaction costs, and enhancing liquidity. Benefiting from a series of policy initiatives over time, greater domestic market integration has also been witnessed.

The equity, government securities, foreign exchange and money markets along with their corresponding derivatives segments have developed into reasonably deep and liquid markets and there has been significant increase in domestic market integration over the years. However, the credit derivative market is yet to take off in any significant manner. As regards corporate bonds, though the primary market has seen an increase in issuance, the secondary market has not developed commensurately.

Financial markets in India are regulated and supervised by the Reserve Bank of India (RBI) and the Securities and Exchange Board of India (SEBI). Financial markets under the purview of the RBI include the following:

1. Money market and derivatives.
2. Foreign exchange market and derivatives.
3. Government securities market and interest rate derivatives.
4. Credit markets and derivatives.

   Financial markets under the control and supervision of SEBI are as under:

1. Equity market and derivatives.
2. Corporate bond market.

11.4 Financial Markets and Monetary Policy of RBI

From the point of view of RBI, developed financial markets are critical for effective transmission of monetary policy impulses to the rest of the economy. Monetary transmission cannot take place without efficient price discovery, particularly with respect to interest rates and exchange rates. The transmission process for policy actions by RBI involves two stages. In the first stage, policy actions are transmitted to financial markets. The second stage of the transmission mechanism involves the propagation of monetary policy impulses from the financial system to the real economy and aggregate prices. A successful implementation of policy requires a reasonably accurate assessment of how rapidly the effects of policy actions are transmitted through the financial system to the real economy, affecting aggregate spending decisions of households and firms, and from there to aggregate demand and inflation.

As a debt manager to the Government, the development of a deep and liquid market for government securities is of critical importance to the RBI as it results in better price discovery and cost effective Government borrowing. The government securities market also provides an effective transmission mechanism for monetary policy, facilitates the introduction and pricing of hedging products and serves as a benchmark for pricing other debt instruments. Although the government securities market has developed considerably over the years, more needs to be done for it to become fully developed.

11.5 Reforms in the Financial Markets

Financial markets in India have existed for a long time. However, they remained relatively underdeveloped for a variety of reasons. India introduced financial sector reforms as a part of structural reforms in the early 1990s. Several measures have been taken by regulatory authorities to develop and strengthen India's financial system in order to make it compatible with best international practices.

Reforms in the financial markets encompassed all segments—money market, credit market, government securities market, foreign exchange market, equity market and corporate debt market. The development of financial markets in India has been pursued to bring about a transformation in the structure, efficiency and stability of markets as also to facilitate integration of markets. The emphasis has been on strengthening price discovery, easing of restrictions on flows or transactions, lowering of transaction costs, and enhancing liquidity. Development of these markets has been done in a calibrated, sequenced and careful manner in step with those in other markets in the real economy. The sequencing has also been informed by the need to develop market infrastructure, technology and capabilities of market participants and financial institutions in a consistent manner. In a low income economy like India, the cost of downside risk is very high, so the objective of maintaining financial stability has to be constantly kept in view while developing financial markets.

The objectives of developing financial markets are as under:

1. To encourage competitive forces.
2. To facilitate the use of a variety of instruments.
3. To promote the growth of different kinds of institutions offering a wide range of financial instruments and services to potential savers and investors.
4. To protect the interests of savers by reducing their risks.
5. To promote the development of instruments that help in risk management.

For regulating financial markets, regulators are guided by various considerations in the larger interest of society. Broadly, the objective of regulation is to protect the interests of depositors and investors (safety and conduct of business), promote financial inclusion, ensure monetary and financial stability and achieve sustained economic progress.

During the post-reforms period, the structure of financial markets has witnessed a remarkable change in terms of financial instruments traded in various segments of the financial market and market participants.

Reforms in the financial markets have encompassed all segments. The development of financial markets in India has been pursued to bring about a transformation in the structure, efficiency and stability of the markets as also to facilitate their integration. The emphasis has been on strengthening price discovery, easing restrictions on flows or transactions, lowering transaction costs, and enhancing liquidity. During the post-reform period, the structure of financial markets has witnessed a significant change in terms of financial instruments traded in various segments of the financial market and market participants. The development of these markets has been done in a calibrated, sequenced and careful manner in step with those in other markets in the real economy. Sequencing has also been informed by the need to develop market infrastructure, technology and the capabilities of market participants and financial institutions in a consistent manner.

The gradual removal of structural bottlenecks in the Indian financial markets and a shift away from the erstwhile administered rates has led to greater domestic market integration. This has also benefited from a series of other policy initiatives over time which included enabling market-determined price discovery through interest rate deregulation; expansion and diversification of the investor base; introduction of a variety of instruments of varying features and tenor; and improvement in market infrastructure. Some of the markets which show strong co-movement are money and government securities markets, exchange rate and stock markets, and foreign exchange forward and money markets.

The need to further develop financial markets has also been underlined by the two high-powered committees, *viz.* Committee on Fuller Capital Account Convertibility (FCAC) [1] and the High Powered Expert Committee on Making Mumbai an International Financial Centre. [2] The Committee on Fuller Capital Account Convertibility in its Report submitted in July 2006 indicated that in order to make a move towards fuller capital account convertibility, it needs to be ensured that different financial market segments are not only well-developed but also that they are well-integrated. Otherwise, shocks to one or more market segments would not get transmitted to other segments efficiently so that the entire financial system is able to absorb the shocks with minimal damage.

To sum up, Indian financial markets can be broadly categorised into the money market, government securities market, equity market, corporate bond market, credit market and foreign exchange market. While equity, government securities, foreign exchange and money markets along with their corresponding derivatives segments have developed into reasonably deep and liquid markets, credit derivatives markets are yet to take off in any significant manner. As regards corporate bonds, while primary issuances have been significant, though concentrated in terms of issuers to public sector financial institutions, these have largely been on a private placement basis and the secondary market has not developed commensurately.

In an emerging market like India, where the cost of downside risk is very high, the objective of maintaining financial stability has always been kept in view while developing financial markets. Financial intermediaries like banks have also gained from better determination of interest rates in financial markets by pricing their own products better. Moreover, their own risk management has also improved through the availability of different varieties of financial instruments. The access of real sector entities to finance has also been assisted by the appropriate development of the financial market and the availability of transparent information on benchmark interest rates and prevailing exchange rates.

Though several reform measures have recently been initiated to develop the financial markets in India, resulting in various segments of the financial market being better developed and integrated, the financial markets need to develop further in line with the evolving financial and economic scenario.

These developments have facilitated the growth of deeper and more efficient domestic markets, facilitating a more effective channel for transmission of monetary and financial policy impulses. India's experience once again demonstrates that the development of financial markets is an arduous and time-consuming task that requires conscious policy actions and effective implementation. Financial markets have to be created, nurtured and monitored on a continuous basis, as they attain maturation.

Endnotes

1. Reserve Bank of India, *Report of the Committee on Fuller Capital Account Convertibility* (Chairman: S.S. Tarapore), 2006.
2. Government of India, *High Powered Expert Committee Report on Making Mumbai an International Financial Centre*, April 2007.

12

Money Market

Money market is the most important segment of the financial system as it provides the fulcrum for equilibrating short-term demand for and supply of funds, thereby facilitating the conduct of monetary policy.

12.1 Meaning and Functions of Money Market

Money market is a market for short-term funds with a maturity of up to one year and includes financial instruments that are close substitutes for money. [1] The main instruments comprising the money market are: (a) call money/notice money, (b) certificates of deposit (CDs), (c) treasury bills (abolished with effect from April 1997), (d) repurchase agreements (repos), (e) commercial bills, (f) commercial paper (CPs), and (g) inter-corporate funds.

While inter-bank money markets and central bank lending via repo operations or discounting, provide liquidity for banks, private non-bank money market instruments, such as commercial bills and commercial paper provide liquidity to the commercial sector. Unlike in developed economies where money markets are promoted by financial intermediaries out of efficiency considerations, in India, as in many other developing countries, the evolution of the money market and its structure has been integrated into the overall deregulation process of the financial sector.

The money market is generally expected to perform three broad functions.

1. It provides an equilibrating mechanism to even out demand for and supply of short-term funds.
2. It also presents a focal point for central bank intervention for influencing liquidity and general level of interest rates

in the economy.

3. It provides reasonable access to providers and users of short-term funds to fulfil their borrowing and investment requirements at an efficient market clearing price.

12.2 RBI and the Money Market

The RBI is the most important constituent of the money market. Owing to its implications for conducting monetary policy, the money market falls under the direct purview of regulation of the RBI. The primary objective of the RBI's operations in the money market has been to ensure that short-term interest rates and liquidity are maintained at levels which are consistent with the overall monetary policy objectives, viz. maintaining price stability, ensuring adequate flow of credit to the productive sectors of the economy and maintaining orderly conditions in the financial markets. Liquidity and interest rates in the system are influenced by the RBI through the use of various instruments at its disposal which, *inter alia*, include the following.

1. Variations in cash reserve ratio.
2. Standing facilities/refinance schemes.
3. Repo and reverse repo transactions.
4. Changes in the Bank Rate.
5. Open market operations.
6. Foreign exchange swap operations.

Recognising the important role of the market in the monetary policy process, the RBI has taken active interest in continuously refining the money market instruments in order to have greater control over the liquidity in the system and for creating an efficient mechanism to impart interest rate signals.

12.3 Evolution of Money Market in India

12.3.1 Pre-Independence Period: Money market prior to Independence was characterised by paucity of instruments, lack of depth and dichotomy in the market structure. The inter-bank call money market was the core of the Indian money market. Before the establishment of the RBI in 1935, the money market consisted of two fairly distinct sectors, *viz*. the organised and unorganised sectors. While the organised sector consisted of the Imperial Bank of India—a quasi-central bank till 1935, [2] the Indian joint-stock banks and the exchange banks, the indigenous bankers such as the shroffs, money lenders, chit funds etc. formed the unorganised part. Co-operative credit institutions occupied an intermediate position between the two sectors.

The Imperial Bank, the foremost commercial bank of the country and a few of the leading Indian joint-stock banks discounted *hundis* (internal bills of exchange). This was the main credit instrument of the unorganised sector which provided the only link between the two sectors. Owing to the absence of a proper central bank, the money market was characterised by sharp imbalances between the supply and demand for funds, wide fluctuations in interest rates during the busy and slack seasons and marked regional variations in interest rates. The Imperial Bank could not, however, lend stability to the money market as it had to borrow from the Government at high rates of interest. Nevertheless, the bank rendered assistance to the money market by using the large Government balances at its disposal, which constituted its major investible resources.

The Bank Rate was the prime lending rate at which the Imperial Bank generally advanced money against Government securities. This rate was determined by the Committee of the Central Board of the Imperial Bank and depended on the demand for money which in turn was determined almost entirely by the requirements of trade, particularly foreign trade, in staple commodities such as foodgrains, raw cotton, raw jute and jute manufactures. The rates of interest on loans, including the Bank Rate, fluctuated according to the ebb and flow of this trade. The Imperial Bank would usually not reduce the Bank Rate when its cash to liabilities ratio (an indication of liquidity) was found to be low.

Apart from the Bank Rate, the Imperial Bank also periodically announced a *hundi* rate, which was generally equal to or slightly higher than the Bank Rate. Through the rates which the Imperial Bank charged on its advances and the discount of *hundis,* and by its willingness or refusal to extend financial assistance, it could profoundly influence the provision of credit as well as money market rates.

After the formation of the RBI in 1935, the organised market comprised the RBI, the Imperial Bank, foreign banks and the Indian joint stock banks. [3] *Quasi*-Government bodies and large-sized joint stock companies also participated in the money market as lenders, the money lent by them being usually termed as *house money*. Financial intermediaries such as call loan brokers, general finance and stock brokers also functioned in the market. Although the magnitude of funds dealt within the call market was not large in relation to the deposit resources of banks, it was the most sensitive segment of the money market. The Imperial Bank did not participate in the call money market, but other banks obtained loans and advances from it. Subsequently, however, banks increasingly shifted their demand for accommodation to the RBI. Besides the call money market, there was no other significant segment in the market.

With the establishment of the RBI in April 1935, the task of determining the Bank Rate was taken over by it from the Imperial Bank. It was on July 4, 1935, i.e. the day before the scheduled banks were to lodge their statutory deposits with the RBI, that the Bank Rate of 3.5 percent was officially announced for the first time by the RBI. It was the standard rate at which the RBI was prepared to buy or re-discount bills of exchange or other eligible commercial papers. Subsequently, the official rate of the Imperial Bank was re-designated as the Imperial Bank advance rate (as distinct from the Imperial Bank *hundi* rate), which was to be the rate for advances against Government securities and the benchmark for the calculation of interest on other advances on which a fluctuating rate of interest was charged.

12.3.2 Post-Independence Period: At the time of Independence in 1947, money market structure in India was loose though not entirely uncoordinated. The indigenous bankers enjoyed rediscount facilities from the Imperial Bank and other commercial banks which, in turn, had access to the RBI. Recourse on the part of the indigenous money market to the resources of the organised market took place usually during the busy season when the crops were being harvested and moved from the producer to the wholesaler.

Though the RBI was empowered, under the statute, to use the usual instruments of monetary policy, the choice of the instruments of monetary control that could be used was limited by the structural characteristics of the money market. An important aspect of the money market in India was the seasonality in the demand for money and credit which broadly followed the course of the agricultural season. The incidence of closing of accounts of the Government at the end of the financial year in March also added to the element of seasonality in the money market.

The introduction of Bill Market Scheme by the RBI on January 16, 1952 was a landmark in the growth of money market in India. [4] Under the scheme, the RBI made advances to scheduled banks in the form of demand loans against their promissory notes supported by 90 days usance bills or promissory notes of their constituents. It was primarily a scheme for providing accommodation to banks. The scheme, however, did not succeed in developing a market in genuine bills.

In order to serve the economy in general and the rural sector in particular, the All-India Rural Credit Survey Committee recommended the creation of the state-partnered and state-sponsored bank by taking over the Imperial Bank of India, and integrating with it, the former state-owned or state-associate banks. An Act was, accordingly, passed in the Parliament in May 1955 and the State Bank of India was constituted on July 1, 1955.

A new scheme called the Bills Rediscounting Scheme was

introduced with several new features in November 1970 under which the RBI rediscounted genuine trade bills at the Bank Rate or at a rate specified by it, at its discretion. Over the years the rediscounting facility was made restrictive and made available on a discretionary basis. The other instrument in the money market was participation certificates (introduced in 1970). Both of these were, however, not significant.

Prior to financial sector reforms initiated in early 1990s, money market in India was characterised by poor liquidity, the paucity of instruments and limited number of participants. The major features of the Indian money market were the following.

1. Restricted market with a narrow base and limited number of participants—banks and two all-India financial institutions. The entry into the market was tightly regulated. Moreover, the market was lopsided with a few large lenders and a large number of borrowers. The market lacked participants who could make for an active market by alternating between lending and borrowing.
2. The overall size of the market was also very small relative to the size of the economy—overall transactions barely formed 3 to 4 percent of the bank deposits.
3. The market was also characterised by paucity of instruments and dealings were generally confined to overnight call and short notice (up to 14 days), inter-bank deposits/loans, Repo market and bills rediscounting.
4. The interest rates in the market were also tightly regulated and controlled [by a voluntary agreement between the participants through the Indian Banks' Association (IBA) intermediation]. However, during periods of tight liquidity, the prescribed rates were not strictly adhered to, and more often breached.

Owing to the above features, the unorganised money market used to meet the sectoral financing gaps (i.e. the requirements of unsatisfied borrowers in the organised financial system). Interest rates in the unorganised sector were higher than those in the organised sector and were more market-related.

The Committee to Review the Working of the Monetary System in India (Chairman: Sukhamoy Chakravarty), 1985 first underlined the need to develop money market instruments in India, while the Working Group on the Money Market (Chairman: N. Vaghul), 1987 laid the blueprint for the institution of money markets. Based on the recommendations of the Chakravarty Committee and the Vaghul Working Group, the RBI has gradually developed money market in India through the following measures.

First, interest rate ceilings on inter-bank call/notice money (10 percent), inter-bank term money (10.5-11.5 percent), rediscounting of commercial bills (12.5 percent) and inter-bank participation without risk (12.5 percent) were withdrawn effective May 1, 1989.

Secondly, several financial innovations in terms of money market instruments, such as auctions of Treasury Bills (beginning with the introduction of 182-day Treasury Bills effective November 1986), certificates of deposit (June, 1989), commercial paper (January 1990) and RBI repo (December 1992) were introduced.

Thirdly, barriers to entry were gradually eased by: (a) increasing the number of players (beginning with the Discount and Finance House of India (DFHI) in April 1988 followed by primary and satellite dealers and money market mutual funds), (b) relaxing both issuance restrictions and subscription norms in respect of money market instruments and allowing determination of yields based on demand and supply of such paper, and (c) enabling market evaluation of associated risks, by withdrawing regulatory restrictions such as bank guarantees in respect of CPs.

Fourthly, the development of markets for short-term funds at market determined interest rates has been fostered by a gradual switch from a cash credit system to a loan-based system, shifting the onus of cash management from banks to borrowers and phasing out the 4.6 percent 91-day tap Treasury bills, which in the past provided an avenue for investing short-term funds.

Finally, institutional development has been carried out to facilitate inter-linkages between the money market and the foreign exchange market, especially after a market-based exchange rate system was put in place in March 1993.

12.4 Developments in the Money Market since 1991

The money market in India witnessed significant progress particularly from the mid-1990s, in terms of refinements in money market instruments, introduction of new instruments and supplementary measures to add depth and liquidity to the market.

During the 1990s, the participation in the call money market was widened to cover primary and satellite dealers and corporates (through primary dealers) besides other participants. While banks and primary dealers are permitted to lend and borrow in the market, other entities can participate only as lenders. Following the recommendations of the Committee on Banking Sector Reforms (Chairman: M. Narasimham), 1998 and the RBI's Internal Working Group to Examine the Development of Call Money Market (1997), steps were initiated to reform the call money market and make it a pure inter-bank market, in a phased manner starting in 1999. With the development of the repo market since the late 1990s, the call money market has gradually been transformed into a pure inter-bank market including primary dealers. This process, which was initiated in 1999, was completed in August 2005.

A significant development in the Indian money market has been the introduction of Rupee derivatives, i.e. interest rate swaps (IRS)/forward rate agreements (FRA) in 1999 to further deepen the money market and enable market participants to hedge their risks. In addition to several other measures taken since its introduction, with effect from May 20, 2005, market participants were advised to use only domestic Rupee benchmarks for interest rate derivatives. Market participants were, however, given a transition period of six months for using Mumbai inter-bank forward offered rate (MIFOR) as a benchmark, subject to review. However, on request from the

Fixed Income Money Market and Derivatives Association (FIMMDA), market participants have been allowed to use MIFOR swaps in respect of transactions having underlying permissible forex exposures, for market making purpose, subject to appropriate limit as may be approved by the RBI.

Following the recommendations of the Technical Group on Money Market (May 2005), the focus and policy thrust of the RBI in the money market has been towards encouraging the growth of collateralised market, ensuring transparency and better price discovery, providing avenues for better risk management and strengthening monetary operations.

Trading in money market instruments can take place on a trading platform or in the OTC market. Electronic platforms are available for deals in the call, notice and term money market transactions, market repo and collateralised borrowing and lending obligation (CBLO). OTC deals are done for commercial paper (CP) and certificate of deposit (CD), as well as for call/notice/term money markets. Settlement is done over the real time gross settlement system—either as a gross settlement or as a multilateral netted batch. CP and CD deals, which are mostly in the form of private placements, are done OTC.

The RBI's regulatory powers over money market securities was strengthened under Clause 45 (W) of the RBI Amendment Act, 2006, wherein the RBI was given specific powers to 'regulate the financial system of the country to its advantage, determine the policy relating to interest rates or interest rate products, and give directions on that behalf to all agencies or any of them, dealing in securities, money market instruments, foreign exchange, derivatives, or other instruments of like nature as the Bank may specify from time to time'.

12.5 Component-wise Analysis of Money Market in India

12.5.1 Call/Notice Money Market: The call money market is an important segment of the money market where uncollateralized borrowing and lending of funds take place on overnight basis. Presently, participants in the call money market in India include scheduled commercial banks (excluding regional rural banks), cooperative banks (other than land development banks), and primary dealers, both as borrowers and lenders. Prudential limits in respect of both outstanding borrowing and lending transactions in the call money market for each of these entities are specified by the RBI.

Money market in India comprises mainly of the call money market. Although other money market segments, viz. commercial bills market and inter-corporate deposits market have been in existence for a long time, there has not been much activity in these segments. Therefore, for assessing the impact of reforms on the money market, the focus is mainly on the call money market. The impact of reforms is assessed in terms of behaviour of the call money market and the market growth related parameters, including those instruments which were introduced in the 1990s.

Call money market deals in overnight funds. Notice money market deals in funds for 2 to 14 days. The call/notice money market serves the purpose of equilibrating the short-term liquidity position of banks and other participants. In order to modulate short-term liquidity under diverse market conditions, the Government introduced a full-fledged liquidity adjustment facility (LAF) on June 5, 2000. Under this scheme, the RBI can adjust market liquidity on a daily basis through repo/reverse repo auctions of varying frequencies. This has emerged as an effective instrument to facilitate overnight call rate movement, resulting in stability and orderly market conditions.

The overnight inter-bank call money market, in which banks trade positions to maintain cash reserves, is the key segment of the money market in India. It is basically an over the counter (OTC) market without the intermediation of brokers. Participation has been gradually widened to include other financial institutions, primary/satellite dealers, mutual funds and other participants in the bills rediscounting market and corporates (through primary dealers) besides banks, LIC and UTI. While banks and primary dealers are allowed two-way operations, other non-bank entities can only participate as lenders. As per the announced policies, once the repo market develops, the call money market would be made into a pure inter-bank market, including primary dealers.

On the supply side, the call money market is influenced by liquidity conditions mainly governed by deposit mobilisation, capital flows and the RBI's operations affecting banks' reserve requirements. On the demand side, it is influenced by tax outflows, government borrowing programme, non-food credit off-take and seasonal fluctuations, such as large currency withdrawals during the festival season. In times of easy liquidity, call rates tend to hover around the RBI's repo rate, which provides a ready avenue for parking short-term surplus funds. During periods of tight liquidity, call rates tend to move up towards the Bank Rate and more recently the RBI's reverse repo rate as the RBI modulates liquidity in pursuit of monetary stability.

Besides, there are other influences such as: (a) reserve requirement prescriptions (and stipulations regarding average reserve maintenance), (b) investment policy of non-bank participants in the call market which are among the large suppliers of funds in the call market, and (c) asymmetries of the call money market, with few lenders and chronic borrowers.

The turnover in the call/notice money market depends on the amount of surplus funds available with some participants and the requirements of funds by some other participants. Over the years, the number of participants in the market has gradually increased to include banks and primary dealers both as lenders and borrowers, and select mutual funds, insurance companies, development financial institutions and corporates through primary dealers (as lenders).

The call money market, the dominant market, was strictly an inter-bank market till 1971 when the UTI and LIC were allowed to operate in the market. While commercial and cooperative banks participated as both lenders and borrowers, LIC and UTI, institutions with a sizeable short-term float funds, were permitted to lend in order to augment the supply of funds in the market. The overnight call/term money had traditionally facilitated banks in maintaining reserve requirements. Thus, in the 1970s and 1980s, call money market in India remained basically "an over the counter (OTC) market" as brokers were not permitted in the market.

Prior to December 1973, the call market rates were freely determined by the market but as the rates touched a high of 25 to 30 percent and remained at that level, the Indian Banks' Association (IBA) intervened and brought some order in the market as it was felt that high interest rate over long periods would distort the entire banking system operations and would also militate against the basic objectives of planned credit allocation under an administered structure of lending rates. A ceiling of 15 percent on call money rate was fixed by the IBA in December 1973; the ceiling was, however, reduced in phases to 8.5 percent by March 1978. The resurgence of inflationary pressures and the sharp upward movement in administered interest rates in 1979-80 necessitated increase in the ceiling on call rates to 10 percent in April 1980.

In the initial phase of money market reforms in the late 1980s, considerable volatility was noticed in the call rate, resulting primarily from a free call money market, while interest rates in other segments of the money market remained regulated. As a result, any fluctuation in the liquidity conditions impinged on the call money market.

The call money market during the 1990s witnessed orderly conditions barring a few episodes of volatility. The call rates first came under pressure in May 1992 when they touched a peak of 35.3 percent, essentially reflecting liquidity tightness due to high levels of statutory pre-emptions and withdrawal of all reliance facilities except for export credit refinance. After witnessing tranquil conditions during July 1992 until December 1994, the call money market came under pressure again during 1995-96. The call rate touched a peak of around

35 percent in November 1995, largely mirroring turbulence in the foreign exchange market. To stabilise the market, the RBI injected liquidity through reverse repos, enhanced banks' refinance facilities against government securities and reduced the CRR. The call rate softened to a single digit level thereafter till December 1997.

However, the call rate hardened again and touched a high of around 29 percent, in January 1998, reflecting the mopping up of money market liquidity by the RBI to ease the pressure in the foreign exchange market. During 1999-2000, the inter-bank call money rates ruled steady within a narrow range, except for a few bouts of volatility, primarily attributable to the unanticipated demand for reserves by commercial banks.

Thus, for a few episodes of volatility, conditions in the call money market remained stable in the 1990s. The full-fledged liquidity adjustment facility (LAF), which was introduced on June 5, 2000, with a view to modulating short-term liquidity under diverse market conditions, emerged as an effective instrument to provide a corridor for the overnight call rate movement. The LAF combined with strategic open market operations (OMOs), has since been used to signal the monetary stance by removing shortfalls and excesses of liquidity in the system so as to keep short-term interest rates reasonably stable.

Over the years, a few banks tended to be overtly exposed to the call/notice money market. Such banks relied excessively on the call money market for carrying out banking operations and long-term asset creation. The Committee on Banking Sector Reforms (Chairman: M. Narasimham), 1998 recommended that there must be clearly defined prudent limits beyond which banks should not be allowed to rely on the call/notice money market and that access to this market should essentially be for meeting unforeseen mismatches and not as regular means of financing lending operations of banks. With progressive regulations, asset liability management system was put in place, which kept the mismatches in cash flows in the 1-28 days bucket under check.

As part of streamlining the LAF and improving the

transmission channel of monetary policy, the phasing out of non-bank participants from the call money market commenced from May 2001. Furthermore, recognising that building up of substantial exposure to the call/notice money market relative to the balance-sheet size by some participants on a continuous basis has the potential not only for default and the consequent systemic instability, but also for impeding other segments of the money market, participants are now operating within limits on both lending and borrowing operations. Thus, the call/notice money market is evolving as a pure inter-bank market with ALM discipline for participants and prudential limits for borrowing and lending.

With the establishment of the Clearing Corporation of India Ltd. (CCIL) and the enhanced liquidity in the repo market both in government and non-government securities, it is envisaged that eventually both the call market and the repo market, combined with other money market instruments, would constitute an integrated market for equilibrating short-term funds for both, banks and non-banks.

12.5.2 Commercial Paper (CP): CP was introduced as a money market instrument in January 1990. The purpose was to enable the companies to diversify their sourcing of short-term borrowings. It also provided investors with an additional instrument for investment.

CP is issued by non-banking companies and all-India financial institutions (AIFIs) as an unsecured promissory note or in a dematerialised form at a rate of discount not tied to any transaction. It is privately placed with investors through the agency of banks. Banks act as both principals (i.e. as counter parties in purchases and sales) and agents in dealership and placement.

Conditions relating to issuing of CPs have been relaxed gradually with a view to broad-basing the market. For instance, the maturity period has been changed from 91 days to 6 months from the earlier 15 days up to 1 year. The minimum size of CPs has also been reduced from ₹ 1 crore to ₹ 5 lakh. The issuer base has been widened by allowing PDs, SDs and AIFIs, apart from corporates, to issue CPs to access short-term funds.

The limit for issuance of CP, which was initially carved out of the maximum permissible bank finance (MPBF), was later linked to the cash credit component of MPBF. With the cash credit component gradually shrinking and, thereby, restricting the development of CP, the issuance limit was delinked from the cash credit limit in October 1997. Initially, banks were required to restore the cash credit limit on the maturity of the paper, guaranteeing the issuer funds at the point of redemption. This *stand-by* facility was withdrawn in October 1994 to impart a measure of independence to CP as a money market instrument.

The pricing of CP usually lies between the scheduled commercial banks' lending rate and some representative money market rate. The Indian CP market is driven by the demand for CP by scheduled commercial banks, which in turn is governed by bank liquidity. Banks' investments in CP, despite a positive interest rate differential between the bank loan rate and the CP rate, may be explained by two factors, viz.: (i) the higher transaction costs of bank loans, and (ii) the relative profitability of CP as an attractive short-term instrument to park funds during times of high liquidity.

As inter-bank call rates are typically lower than the CP rates, some banks also fund CP by borrowing from the call money market and thus book profit through arbitrage between the two money markets. Most of the CPs seem to have been issued by the manufacturing companies for a maturity period of approximately 3 months or less, mainly due to the fact that investors do not wish to lock funds for long periods of time.

Secondary activity is subdued in most CP markets on account of the investors' preference to hold the instrument due to higher risk-adjusted returns relative to those of other instruments. However, mutual funds find the secondary market relatively remunerative, since stamp duty for the issuer will be higher in case the buyer is a mutual fund rather than a bank.

Hence, there is a tendency to route a CP through an institution (usually a bank), which attracts lower stamp duty in the primary market, to a mutual fund in the secondary market.

The Indian CP market is driven by swings in bank liquidity. Banks prefer investing in CPs especially in times of easy liquidity as they can park funds at interest rates higher than call rates and at the same time avoid higher transaction costs associated with bank loans. The effective discount rate of CP usually lies between representative money market rate and the bank lending rate. On the other hand, companies are able to raise funds through CPs at a lower rate than the lending rates of banks under easy liquidity conditions.

Further measures to spur the CP market have included conversion of CP into a stand-alone product in October 2000, trading of CPs in dematerialised form (which helped to lower transaction costs) and reduction in stamp duty effective March 1, 2004.

12.5.3 Certificates of Deposit (CDs): CDs were introduced in 1989 as a money market instrument to mobilise large value deposits. Such deposits were freed from interest rate regulations in 1992. Banks can now have the option to meet their liquidity needs through these certificates issued at a premium during tight liquidity conditions.

CDs are essentially securitised short-term time deposits issued by banks during periods of tight liquidity, at relatively high interest rates (in comparison with term deposits). But the transaction cost of CDs is often lower as compared with that of retail deposits. When credit picks up, placing pressure on banks' liquidity, banks try to meet their liquidity gap by issuing CDs, often at a premium. The required amounts are mobilised in larger amounts through CDs, often for short periods in order to avoid interest liability overhang in the subsequent months when credit demand slackens. As banks offer higher interest rates on CDs, subscribers find it profitable to hold CDs till maturity. As a result, the secondary market for CDs has been slow to develop.

The steady increase of CDs has been on account of several factors.

1. Revised guidelines by the RBI on investments by banks in non-SLR debt securities.
2. Reduction in stamp duty on CDs effective March 1, 2004.
3. Withdrawal of tax deduction at source.
4. Disallowing premature closure of deposits under CDs.
5. Greater opportunity for secondary market trading.

On the demand side, the Securities and Exchange Board of India (SEBI) placing a bar on mutual funds (MFs) from parking funds in bank deposits coupled with improved funds position with MFs provided an impetus to the CD market. An encouraging development in the CD market is that some of the top-rated banks have been getting their CDs rated for better access to the market even when such rating is not mandatory under the extant guidelines.

12.5.4 Repos: Repo (repurchase agreement) is a money market instrument, which enables collaboralised short-term borrowing and lending through sale/purchase operations in debt instruments. Under a repo transaction, a holder of securities sells them to an investor with an agreement to repurchase at a pre-determined date and rate. In the case of a repo, the forward clean price of the bonds is set in advance at a level which is different from the spot clean price by adjusting the difference between repo interest and coupon earned on the security. Repo is also called a ready forward transaction as it is a means of funding by selling a security held on a spot (ready) basis and repurchasing the same on a forward basis. Reverse repo is a mirror image of repo as in the case of former, securities are acquired with a simultaneous commitment to resell.

In India, banks often entered into buy back arrangements in respect of Government and other approved securities and PSU bonds among themselves and with their large public sector and corporate clients until April 15, 1987 when the RBI issued certain guidelines prohibiting buy back arrangements in respect of corporate securities and bonds issued by public sector undertakings. From December 1, 1987 the units of Unit Trust of India were not eligible as approved security for the purpose of entering into repo transactions. In order to ward off any undesirable developments following the detection of large scale misuse of repos, banks were prohibited from entering into buy back arrangements in Government and other approved securities with non-bank clients, while they could enter into buy-back arrangements with other banks (inter-bank) with effect from April 4, 1988.

The repo market suffered a major setback due to the securities irregularities of 1992. The Janakiraman Committee, set up in the wake of the securities market irregularities reported that there existed a thriving market for repos and virtually all wholesale participants of the money market and not only banks, used repo transactions widely, despite there being an explicit prohibition on their use. After the detection of the irregularities, the RBI imposed a ban on ready forward deals and banks were prohibited from undertaking repos in Government dated securities and approved/trustee securities from June 22, 1992. Repos in Treasury Bills were, however, exempted from prohibition. Double ready forward deals, including those in Treasury Bills were also strictly prohibited and the ban was extended to financial institutions as well.

Justice Variava's judgement was of great significance in the context of development of the repo market in India as it held that all repo transactions undertaken by banks and other institutions were illegal and void as they were prohibited under Section 16 of the Securities Contract Regulation Act (SCRA), 1956 and Government's notification dated June 27, 1969. In order to legally facilitate the repo transactions, the RBI had to take up the issue with the Government to exempt banks and such of those entities deemed necessary by the RBI, from the prohibition contained in the notification.

Amending the Notification which prohibited forward transactions in securities, the Government issued notifications by virtue of which banking companies, co-operative banks, primary dealers (by name) and satellite dealers (by name) were permitted to undertake ready forward transactions in specified securities, provided the transactions were settled through SGL Accounts maintained at the Public Debt Office, Mumbai. Further, non-bank entities as notified by the Central Government were permitted to undertake reverse repos only.

Following the recommendations of the Committee on Banking Sector Reforms (Chairman: M. Narasimham), 1998, an interim liquidity adjustment facility (ILAF) was introduced initially in April 1999. This later translated into a full-fledged LAF, put in place on June 5, 2000. Under this arrangement, the RBI was able to adjust market liquidity on a daily basis through repo/reverse repo auctions of varying frequencies under the LAF. Though the interest rates in the repo/reverse repo auctions usually emerge out of the bids, the RBI occasionally conducts fixed rate auctions to send signals to the market. Hence, the interest rates emerging out of the repo and reverse repo auctions provide a corridor for call money and other short-term interest rates. The LAF has gradually emerged as the principal operating instrument of monetary policy, replacing all other windows of liquidity support to the market.

In view of the irregularities in securities transactions, repos were initially allowed in Central Government Treasury bills and dated securities, created by converting some of the Treasury bills. In order to activate the repos market, essentially to be an equilibrating force between the money market and the Government securities market, the RBI gradually extended the repos facility to all Central Government dated securities and Treasury Bills of all maturities. Recently, while the State Government securities were made eligible for repos, the RBI also allowed all non-banking entities, maintaining SGL and current accounts with its Mumbai office, to undertake repos (including reverse repos). Furthermore, it was decided to make PSU bonds and private corporate securities eligible for repos to broaden the repos market.

Repo/reverse repo operations are also undertaken by the

RBI as part of its open market operations. The RBI initially conducted repo operations for a period of 14 days. Since November 1996, the RBI has been conducting 3-4 day repo auctions, synchronizing with working day and week-end liquidity conditions, in order to modulate short-term liquidity. With the introduction of liquidity adjustment facility (LAF) from June 5, 2000, the RBI has been injecting liquidity into the system through repos on a daily basis. These operations are conducted on all working days except on Saturdays, through uniform price auctions and are restricted to scheduled commercial banks and PDs.

To develop and widen the repos market, the RBI introduced regulatory safeguards such as delivery versus payments (DvP) system in April 1999. The operationalisation of negotiated dealing system (NDS) and the Clearing Corporation of India Ltd. (CCIL) provided a further boost to this market.

The turnover in the repo market has shown an increasing trend on account of various factors such as limits placed on eligible market participants relating to call/notice money transactions, introduction of DvP III, permitting rollover of repo and market repo rate ruling below the call rate during certain periods. Effective February 23, 2003, based on the advice of the Technical Advisory Committee (TAC) on Money and Government Securities Markets, repo eligibility was extended to select category of non-SGL account holders with adequate safeguards to ensure delivery *versus* payment and transparency. Also effective May 11, 2005, participation in market repo facility has been extended to non-scheduled urban cooperative banks and companies having gilt accounts with scheduled commercial banks, subject to certain eligibility criteria and safeguards.

Being a money market instrument, regulation of the repo market falls under the RBI's jurisdiction. Accordingly, the RBI is concerned with use of repo as an instrument by banks or non-bank entities and issues relating to type of eligible instruments for undertaking repo and eligibility of participants to undertake such transactions. It has been issuing instructions in this regard to banks, in consultation with the Central Government.

12.5.5 Collateralised Borrowing and Lending Obligation (CBLO): It a money market instrument as approved by the RBI. It is a product developed by CCIL for the benefit of entities who have either been phased out from the inter-bank call money market or have been given restricted participation in terms of ceiling on call borrowing and lending transactions and who do not have access to the call money market. CBLO is a discounted instrument available in electronic book entry form for a maturity period ranging from one day to ninety days (can be made available up to one year as per guidelines of RBI).

CBLO is explained as under:

1. An obligation by the borrower to return the money borrowed, at a specified future date.
2. An authority to the lender to receive money lent, at a specified future date with an option/privilege to transfer the authority to another person for value received.
3. An underlying charge on securities held in custody (with CCIL) for the amount borrowed/lent.

12.6 Report of the Technical Group on Money Market

To review the recent developments and current status of money market in the context of evolving monetary policy framework, fiscal scenario, regulatory regime and extent of financial integration, domestic as well as external, a Technical Group on Money Market was constituted. The Group in its Report submitted in May 2005 made several recommendations for furthering the development of the money Market.

The Group recommended that the policy thrust should be to encourage collateralised market, develop the rupee yield curve, ensure transparency and better price discovery, provide avenues for better risk management and strengthen monetary operations. The main recommendations of the Group are set out below.

1. Transactions in the call/notice money market should be conducted on an electronic negotiated quote driven platform.
2. Banks and PDs with appropriate risk management systems in place and balance sheet structure may be allowed more flexibility to borrow in the call/notice money market.
3. Upon accomplishing the call/notice money market into a pure inter-bank one, larger freedom in lending in the call/notice market should be afforded to banks and PDs.
4. Consequent upon coming into effect of the Fiscal Responsibility and Budget Management (FRBM) Act, 2003, there would be a need to broad-base the pool of securities to act as collateral for repo and CBLO markets.
5. The possibility of conducting repo transactions on an electronic, anonymous order driven trading system be explored.
6. Term money market transactions should be compulsorily reported on NDS platform to improve transparency. Term money market transactions on an electronic, negotiated quote driven platform should be introduced.
7. The maturity period of CDs be reduced to 7 days in line with that of CPs and fixed deposits.
8. Asset-backed CPs be introduced in the Indian market.
9. Appropriate amendment to the Reserve Bank of India Act, 1934 be carried out to provide legal clarity to the OTC derivatives.
10. Regulatory issues pertaining to new instruments such as MIBOR-linked short-term papers need to be addressed for an orderly development of the market.
11. Late hour intra-day LAF as and when warranted in future be explored.

12.6.1 Follow-up Action: Certain recommendations of the Group were accepted for implementation and several measures were initiated in the Annual Policy Statement of the RBI announced in April 2005.

In consonance with the declared policy of phased

withdrawal of non-bank participants, barring PDs from the call/notice money market, effective the fortnight beginning June 11, 2005, non-bank participants were allowed to lend, on an average, in a reporting fortnight, up to 10 percent of their average daily lending in the call/notice money market during 2000-01. Effective August 6, 2005 non-bank participants were completely phased out from the call/notice money market. In order to prevent imprudent leveraging of funds, effective April 30, 2005, the benchmark for fixing prudential limits on exposures to the call/notice money market in the case of scheduled commercial banks was linked to their capital funds.

Further steps were taken to broaden the scope of negotiated dealing system (NDS) platform with a view to enhancing transparency and price discovery as also to foster greater market integrity. From April 30, 2005, all NDS members were required to report their term money deals on NDS platform. Further, a screen-based negotiated quote-driven system for all dealings in call/notice and term money market transactions was proposed in the Annual Policy Statement of the RBI for 2005-06. An electronic trading platform for conduct of market repo operations in Government securities, in addition to the existing voice based system, was also proposed. Further, it was proposed to facilitate automated value-free transfer of securities between market participants and the Clearing Corporation of India Ltd. (CCIL) for development of the CBLO segment.

With a view to augmenting the instruments available to banks to manage their liquidity, the minimum maturity period of CDs was reduced from 15 days to 7 days with effect from April 28, 2005. Earlier, in the Mid-term Review of Annual Policy Statement for 2004-05, the minimum maturity period of CP was reduced from 15 days to 7 days with effect from October 26, 2004, in order to provide an option to issuers to raise short-term resources through CP as also an avenue to investors in the form of quality short-term papers.

In order to enhance transparency and facilitate wider dissemination, information on CP issuance, such as issue date, maturity date, issue amount, was made available on the website of the RBI with effect from July 1, 2005.

With a view to harmonising the stamp duty applicable on issuance of CP and bringing the Indian CP market closer to international standard, the Union Budget for 2005-06 proposed to rationalise the stamp duty and apply it uniformly regardless of the initial class of investor.

12.7 Areas of Concern

Although significant progress has been made through initiation of various reforms, there are several issues, which need to be addressed. While the overnight market is reasonably developed, the term-money market is yet to develop necessitating large rollover of short-term funds in the overnight market. This is mainly on account of the inability of participants to form appropriate interest rate expectations in the medium-term due to which there is a tendency on their part to look themselves into a short-term period. Furthermore, overwhelming preference of corporates for *cash* credit rather than for *loan* credit generally forces banks to deploy a large amount in the call/notice money market rather than in the term money market.

Another issue relates to the avenues available to deploy short-term funds to non-bank corporates. A critical issue in transforming the call/notice money market into a pure inter-bank market is the availability of some other avenue for short-term funds for non-bank participants. The commercial bill market continues to be limited, especially as few participants are willing to bear the concomitant risk of default. Thus, the repo trade at this stage offers a quick medium for developing a market for short-term funds especially as the transactions are collateralised in the case of non-banks. While the RBI has taken several steps to develop a repo market for non-bank participants, a vibrant repo market is, however, yet to develop. There is also a need to develop uniform accounting and documentation procedures in this regard.

To sum up, the money market is an important channel for monetary policy transmission and has generally conformed to being a liquid market. The gradual shift towards a collateralised inter-bank market, policy directions towards reductions in statutory reserve requirements, the introduction of new instruments such as CBLO, implementation of RTGS, significant transformation of monetary operations framework towards market-based arrangements and facilitating trading through NDS-CALL are some of the factors that have contributed to the development of a relatively vibrant and liquid money market. However, the inability of market participants to take a medium-to long-term perspective on interest rates and liquidity, coupled with the absence of a credible long-term benchmark, is a major hurdle for further market development and needs to be addressed.

Money market in India, which traditionally consisted largely of call/notice money market, now comprises many other instruments such as CPs, CDs, repos and FRAs/IRS. Various reform measures have helped in improving the depth and efficiency of money market operations. The operationalisation of the LAF has provided an informal corridor for overnight call money borrowing rate, which has further imparted stability and flexibility in the interest rate structure and to the market. The other money market instruments such as CPs and CDs have also been developed through alignment in maturity (with deposit instruments like term deposits) and easing of issuance norms. With proper development of other money market segments, non-banks have been able to smoothly switch over from the call/notice money market to other segments.

The RBI's approach has been to foster balanced development of different segments of the money market, introduce new instruments and make the existing instruments more flexible, reduce dependence of participants on uncollateralised exposures, facilitate price discovery in the short-end and upgrade the payment system infrastructure. Accordingly, the RBI's strategy has focused on developing pure call/notice money market, instituting full-fledged liquidity adjustment facility, developing infrastructure, promoting transparency, and initiating various measures pertaining to instruments for non-bank participants. Following the various initiatives taken by the RBI over the years, the depth and liquidity in the money market has increased significantly.

Historically, the call money market has constituted the core of the money market in India. However, the collateralized segments, viz. market repo and CBLO, have come into prominence recently. Market structure is broad-based with participation of banks, primary dealers, insurance companies, mutual funds, provident funds, and corporates.

Endnotes

1. There is no demarcated distinction between the short-term money market and the long-term capital market, and in fact there are integral links between the two markets as the array of instruments in the two markets invariably forms a continuum.
2. The Imperial Bank acted as the bankers' bank, though not statutorily, till 1935 and held the balances of other banks (both Indian and exchange) and also granted accommodation to them when in difficulty or during periods of tight money conditions. (This position remained unchanged even after 1935 in regions where the RBI had not set up offices). Advances were generally granted by way of demand loans against the Government or other gilt edged securities, though at times these were also in the nature of overdrafts.
3. As early as in 1931, the Indian Central Banking Enquiry Committee (1931) had underscored the need for integration of the two sectors of the Indian money market. It had recommended linking of indigenous bankers satisfying certain conditions such as minimum capital and reserves, nature of business, having audited accounts *etc.*, with the RBI. Subsequently, the RBI drew up a scheme in August 1937 for inclusion of indigenous bankers doing banking business under the Second Schedule of the Reserve Bank of India Act, 1934.

   At around the time the RBI was established, the unorganised money market was the most important segment accounting for as much as 90 percent of the transactions. Since then, its importance in overall terms fell considerably. But for certain sectors such as agriculture, retail trade, various classes of small borrowers and also to an extent small scale industry, this market continued to remain an important source of finance, its chief advantages being flexibility in operations and ease of access to the borrowers. But these advantages were more than offset by the highly onerous terms on which resources were made available to the borrowers. One of the most important objectives of policy at that time was, therefore, to devise methods to facilitate the flow of credit to these sectors from the organised sector and to provide it on reasonable terms.

4. Rediscounting bills were among the most important instruments of credit control and the Indian Central Banking Enquiry Committee (1931) had recommended early establishment of a market in commercial bills. No steps could, however, be taken by the RBI in this direction until the beginning of 1952 because of the War and the difficulties arising out of the partition of the country.

13

Government Securities Market

The government securities market deals with tradable debt instruments issued by the Government for meeting its financing requirements. It is an important segment of the financial market in most countries. The development of the primary segment of this market enables the managers of public debt to raise resources from the market in a cost effective manner with due recognition to associated risks. A vibrant secondary segment of the government securities market helps in the effective operation of monetary policy through application of indirect instruments such as open market operations, for which government securities act as collateral.

Markets for government securities have gained importance in many countries in the overall financial system in recent years. Initiatives have been taken to make them more vibrant and active by: (a) improving liquidity and depth, (b) enhancing transparency of primary issuances, (c) widening investor base, (d) fine-tuning auction procedures, (e) developing new instruments, and (f) putting in place appropriate safeguards and sound trading and settlement infrastructure. Furthermore, managers of public debt across countries are paying greater attention to minimising the cost of borrowings in the medium to long-term, while striking a balance between the costs and the risks in the short-run.

13.1 Meaning of Securities and Government Securities

Under Section 2 of the Securities Contracts (Regulation) Act, 1956, securities include the following:

1. Shares, scrips, stocks, bonds, debentures, debenture stocks, or other marketable securities of a like nature in or of any incorporated company or other body corporate.
2. Government securities.

3. Such other instruments as may be declared by the Central Govt. to be securities.
4. Rights or interests in securities.

Government Securities mean securities created and issued—whether before or after the commencement of the Securities Contracts (Regulations) Act, 1956—by the Central Government or a State Government for the purpose of raising a public loan and having one of the forms specified in Section 2(2) of the Public Debt Act, 1944 (since replaced by the Government Securities Act, 2006).

13.2 Importance of Government Securities Market

Existence of a well-developed government securities market is essential for the pursuit of a market-based monetary policy. The Government securities market in India forms an overwhelming part of the overall debt market. Interest rates in this market provide benchmarks for other segments of the financial market. Historically, the impetus for development of the Government securities market in India has come from the large Government borrowing requirements while an additional reason during the 1990s was the increased capital flows and the need for sterilisation.

As a debt manager to the Government, the development of a deep and liquid market for government securities is of critical importance to the RBI as it results in better price discovery and cost effective Government borrowing. The government securities market also provides an effective transmission mechanism for monetary policy, facilitates the introduction and pricing of hedging products and serves as a benchmark for pricing other debt instruments. Although the government securities market has developed considerably over the years, more needs to be done for it to become fully developed.

The government securities market is also regarded as the backbone of fixed income securities markets as it provides the benchmark yield and imparts liquidity to other financial markets. The existence of an efficient government securities market is seen as an essential precursor, in particular, for development of the corporate debt market. Furthermore, the government securities market acts as a channel for integration of various segments of the domestic financial market and helps in establishing inter-linkages between the domestic and external financial markets.

From the perspective of the issuer, i.e. the Government, a deep and liquid government securities market facilitates its borrowings from the market at reasonable cost. A greater ability of the Government to raise resources from the market at market determined rates of interest allows it to refrain from monetisation of the deficit through central bank funding. It also obviates the need for a captive market for its borrowings. Instead, investor participation is voluntary and based on risk and return perception.

A series of institutional and structural reform measures undertaken in the government securities market since the early 1990s with the objective of creating a deep and liquid market have brought about significant improvements. With the aligning of coupons on government securities with market interest rates, markets gradually widened with the participation of several non-bank players. Presently, investor base includes—apart from banks and insurance companies—private corporate sectors, private sector mutual funds, finance companies as also individuals. Recent steps to allow retailing of government securities and introduction of trading in government securities at stock exchanges are expected to give a further impetus to this trend.

As a result, the market has become deeper and more liquid and the Government is able to mobilise adequate funds from the market. The RBI's absorption of primary issues has come down drastically. Even the limited primary purchases, taken as private placement/development, are off-loaded in the market. This, in turn, has enabled the elimination of automatic monetisation by the RBI and reduction in statutory pre-emption of banks. These arrangements have provided functional autonomy to the RBI in the conduct of monetary policy.

Consequently, a series of structural and institutional reforms, a deep, wide and vibrant gilt market has emerged. The secondary market turnover of government securities in India has been rising steadily, reflecting increased liquidity in the market and increased trading activity by market participants. This sharp increase in turnover was due to a sustained rally in the government securities market.

RBI earlier held Government securities predominantly for supporting the Government borrowing programme as also for conducting open market operations. Banks have been the dominant investors in the Government securities primarily on account of SLR requirements. The investor-base in the Government securities market has widened since the early 1990s, which now comprises commercial banks, cooperative banks, insurance companies, provident funds, financial institutions (including term-lending institutions), mutual funds, gilt funds, primary dealers, non-bank finance companies and corporate entities.

In recent years, it has been found that banks have invested in the Government securities well beyond the statutory requirements partly because of relatively attractive rates of return and zero risk-weight assigned to such investments under capital adequacy norms and partly because of relatively sluggish demand for commercial credit.

13.3 Evolution of Government Securities Market

At the time of Independence in 1947, Government securities market was not significant due mainly to the artificially low coupon rates on Government securities. Financing of the budget deficit of the Central Government by the RBI took place through an arrangement of automatic monetisation through *ad hoc* Treasury Bills. To ensure absorption of the large supply of Government bonds in the face of administered rates, the RBI mandated maintenance of a minimum statutory liquidity ratio (SLR) whereby the commercial banks had to set aside substantial portions of their liabilities for investment in Government securities at below market interest rates. The market was also characterised by several peculiarities such as voucher trading, switch quotas, cash purchase and separate purchase and sale lists. Investors in the gilt-edged securities included individuals as well as financial institutions. Over a period, the gilt-edged market had assumed the nature of captive market with the financial institutions as the major subscribers.

Effective from March 16, 1949, banks had to maintain liquid assets in cash, gold or unencumbered approved securities amounting to not less than 20 percent of their total demand and time liabilities (DTL) under Section 24 of the Banking Regulation Act, 1949. The SLR was the outcome of the action taken to prevent banks from offsetting the impact of variable reserve requirements by liquidating their Government security holdings.

From 1970, the SLR was gradually increased with the objective of restricting the expansionary trend in bank credit as also for augmenting investments of banks in Government securities particularly in the context of financing of the Five Year Plans. The regional rural banks (RRBs) and cooperative banks were permitted to maintain the SLR at the minimum of 25 percent. The SLR was frequently increased in the 1970s touching 34 percent in December 1978, 35 percent in October 1981, and further to 38.5 percent in September 1990. Following the recommendations of the Committee on Financial Sector Reforms (Chairman: M. Narasimham), 1991, SLR was gradually reduced to stand at 25 percent in October 1997. To deal with the global financial crisis—and the consequent need to pump more liquidity in the market—SLR was reduced from 25 percent to 24 percent in November 2008.

13.3.1 Pre-reforms Period: One aspect of the financial market structure in India during the pre-1991 period was the narrowness of the market for Government and semi-Government securities. This meant that there was little scope for using open market operations in Government securities for controlling liquidity. The RBI's operations in this sphere were, therefore, directed mainly at ensuring orderly conditions in the Government securities market so that there was a reasonable allocation of the available resources between the Government sector and the rest of the economy.

The development of the government securities market in India in the pre-reform period was mainly constrained, like in most developing countries, by almost unlimited automatic monetisation of the Central Government budget deficits, captive investors (predominantly banks and insurance companies) and administered coupon rates on government securities at artificially low levels. As a result, the secondary market for government securities was almost non-existent. This impinged on the price discovery process, which is crucial for the development of any market. Since interest rates were kept low in order to ensure low cost of Government borrowing, real rates of return remained negative for several years. Artificially low yields on government securities affected the interest rate structure in the system. In order to compensate for low yield on government securities, banks charged higher interest rates to the commercial sector.

Higher interest rates for the private commercial sector not only adversely impacted investment activity and economic growth, but also affected the financial health of the banking system as bad debts mounted over time. Low economic growth resulted in lower revenues for the Government, both tax and non-tax, necessitating higher borrowing. This was largely met through the mechanism of *ad hoc* Treasury Bills issued by the Government to the RBI and the progressive increase in SLR, as a result of which the government securities market remained dormant. Driven by the compulsions of automatic monetisation, which resulted in expansion of monetary base, the RBI had to progressively raise the cash reserve ratio (CRR) of banks for monetary management. In the face of large government borrowings and the need to restore the health of the financial system, the RBI, in consultation with the Government, initiated reforms in the government securities market as a part of financial sector reforms in the early 1990s. These reforms were broadly aimed at removing the imperfections in the market and creating enabling conditions for its development.

Prior to introduction of reforms, the investor base for government securities consisted of institutions such as banks, financial institutions, provident funds, insurance companies and pension funds, which are statutorily mandated to invest in these securities. To meet the growing financing needs of the Government, the SLR for banks was raised over a period of time to reach the peak rate of 38.5 percent of NDTL in February 1992.

13.4 Post-1991 Measures to Promote Government Securities Market

As the debt manager to the Government, the development of a deep and liquid market for Government securities is of critical importance to the RBI for facilitating the process of price discovery and reducing the cost of Government debt. The RBI has taken several structural and development measures for deepening and widening the Government securities market. In recent years, the approach to the development of Government securities market has focused on greater transparency, risk free settlement, liquidity, and broad-based participation.

Recognising the importance of the government securities market, the RBI, in consultation with the Government, undertook wide-ranging reforms to develop this market. The major objectives of reforms were as follows:

1. To grant operational autonomy to the RBI.
2. To improve institutional infrastructure.
3. To impart liquidity and increase the depth of the market.
4. To improve market microstructure.
5. To create an enabling sound legal and regulatory framework.
6. To increase transparency.

Keeping these objectives in view, reforms were undertaken to strengthen the primary and the secondary segments of the government securities market. In the primary segment, measures were taken to raise resources from the market in a cost effective manner, particularly in the light of the transition to market-related interest rate structure from the administered interest rate regime. In the secondary segment, measures were initiated to improve liquidity in the market. Measures were also undertaken to improve the trading systems, clearing and settlement infrastructure and the risk management framework.

The 1990s marked a watershed in the development of the Government securities market with wide ranging reforms in terms of instruments, institutions and procedures. A major development in the market was the introduction of an auction system for dated securities in June 1992, which marked a move towards market-related rates on the Government securities. Key instruments were also introduced at the longer end of the maturity spectrum with special features to hedge various risks and suit investor preferences during the 1990s. Innovations were also introduced with respect to long-term bonds, such as zero coupon bonds (January 1994), floating rate bonds (1995-96) and capital-indexed bonds (December 1997). Bonds with call and put options were also issued.

Significant steps taken by the RBI in the recent period have included the following.

1. Elongation of maturity.
2. Development of new benchmark Government securities by consolidating new issuances in key maturities.
3. Enhancing fungibility and liquidity by re-issuances of the existing loans.
4. Promoting retailing of Government securities.
5. Introduction of floating rate bonds.
6. Announcement of a calendar for conducting auctions.
7. Enhanced transparency of the Central Government's borrowing programme.

Consequently, the government securities market has witnessed significant transformation in various dimensions, viz. market-based price discovery, widening of investor base, introduction of new instruments, establishment of primary dealers, and electronic trading and settlement infrastructure. This, in turn, has enabled the RBI to perform its functions in tandem with the evolving economic and financial conditions.

Wide-ranging reforms in the government securities market were largely undertaken in response to the changing economic environment. Increased borrowing requirements of the Government, stemming from high fiscal deficits, had to be met in a cost-effective manner without distorting the financial system. The underlying perspective of the reform process was, therefore, to raise government debt at market related rates through an appropriate management of market borrowing. There was also a need to develop a benchmark for other fixed income instruments for purposes of their pricing and valuation. An active secondary market for government securities was also needed for operating monetary policy through indirect instruments such as open market operations and repos. Reforms, therefore, focussed on the development of appropriate market infrastructure, elongation of maturity profile, increasing the width and depth of the market, improving risk management practices and increasing transparency.

As stipulated under the Fiscal Responsibility and Budget Management Act, 2003, the Reserve Bank has withdrawn from participating in the primary market for government securities from April 1, 2006. The increasing move towards fuller capital account convertibility as recommended by the Committee on Fuller Capital Account Convertibility (Chairman: S.S. Tarapore), 2006 would necessitate measures that promote greater integration of the domestic financial markets with global markets. The deepening of the government securities market is, therefore, essential not only for transmission of policy signals but also for developing the derivatives market which would meet future challenges thrown up by further liberalisation of the capital account.

Moreover, an environment of freer capital flows will also necessitate widening of the government securities market with further diversification of the investor base. The RBI is continuing its efforts to further deepen and broaden the Government securities market. A number of initiatives have been taken to modernise the operations relating to Government securities.

13.5 Government Securities Market: Legal Framework and Role of the RBI

RBI, as a monetary authority, has a special interest in developing the government securities market given its criticality in acting as the transmission channel of monetary policy. Moreover, it is important for the RBI, as a manager of public debt, to have a well-developed government securities market as it provides flexibility to exercise various options for optimising maturity as well as interest cost to the Government. It also helps in minimising the market impact of large or lumpy government debt operations and ensuring better coordination between monetary policy and debt management policy. A comprehensive legal framework exists, which defines the role of the RBI in the government securities market.

The legal basis for RBI's operations in the Government securities market is provided by Sections 20, 21 and 21A of the Reserve Bank of India Act, 1934, according to which the RBI is entrusted with the function of management of public debt and issue of new loans of the Union Government and State Governments. The provisions of the Public Debt Act, 1944 (since replaced by the Government Securities Act, 2006) also enjoin upon the RBI the responsibility of administration of the public debt. The functions include issuance of new loans, payment of interest every half year, retirement of rupee loans and all matters pertaining to debt certificates and registration of debt holdings.

RBI actively operates in the gilt-edged market in order to create orderly conditions in the market by influencing the prices and yields of securities. Under Section 17(8) of the Reserve Bank of India Act, 1934, the RBI is authorised to purchase and sell securities of the Union Government or a

State Government of any maturity and the security of a local authority specified by the Central Government on the recommendations of the Central Board of the RBI. In fact, this section provides the legal setting for the conduct of open market operations and liquidity adjustment facility (LAF). Effective April 3, 2007, the State Development Loans were also permitted as eligible securities for LAF operations. The new Chapter III-D of the Reserve Bank of India (Amendment) Act, 2006 has empowered the RBI to determine policy relating to interest rate products and regulate the agencies dealing, *inter alia,* in securities.

However, at present the RBI deals only in the securities issued by the Central Government and not in those of State Governments and local authorities.

RBI derives its regulatory power over the government securities market from Section 16 of the Securities Contract (Regulation) Act (SCRA), 1956, amended in March 2000, under which the Government has delegated the powers exercisable by it to the RBI. The RBI is, thus, authorised to regulate dealings in government securities, money market securities, gold related securities and securities derived from these securities as also ready forward contracts in debt securities.

Government Securities Act, which replaced the Public Debt Act, 1944, was passed in August 2006. This Act envisages the consolidation and amendment of the law relating to issue and management of government securities by the RBI. The Act includes the provisions of the erstwhile Public Debt Act relating to issuance of new loans, payment of half-yearly interest, retirement of rupee loans and all matters pertaining to debt certificates and registration of debt holdings. Besides, the new Act gives flexibility for holding government securities in depositories, while at the same time specifically excluding government securities from the purview of the Depositories Act, 1996. The Act enables lien marking and pledging of securities for raising loans against government securities, recognises electronic form of record maintenance, enlarges dematerialisation facility through Bond Ledger Account and liberalises norms relating to nomination and legal representation.

The Act also provides the RBI with substantive powers to design and introduce an instrument of transfer suited to the computer environment. It also allows the RBI to issue duplicate securities, new securities on conversion, consolidate with other like government securities, strip (separately for interest and principal) or reconstitute the securities.

Apart from the comprehensive legal framework which defines the role of the RBI in the government securities market, there are other agencies which come into the picture. As government securities are listed on the stock exchanges and could be traded through stock exchange brokers, they also come under the regulatory ambit of Securities and Exchange Board of India (SEBI) to that extent. An element of self-regulation is in place through the Fixed Income Money Market and Derivatives Association of India (FIMMDA) and the Primary Dealers Association of India (PDAI), though they are not formally recognised as Self-regulatory Organizations (SROs).

13.6 Mandated Investments in Government Securities: Categories of Investors

Banks are the largest investors in government securities. In terms of the SLR provisions of the Banking Regulation Act, 1949, banks are required to maintain a minimum of 25 percent of their net demand and time liabilities (NDTL) in liquid assets such as cash, gold and unencumbered government securities or other approved securities as statutory liquidity ratio (SLR).

The minimum SLR stipulation for scheduled urban co-operative banks (UCBs) is the same as for scheduled commercial banks (SCBs) from April 1, 2003. However, for non-scheduled UCBs, the minimum SLR requirement is 15 percent for banks with NDTL of over ₹ 25 crore and 10 percent for the remaining non-scheduled UCBs.

The minimum SLR stipulation for regional rural banks

(RRBs) is the same as for SCBs. From April 1, 2003, the coverage under the SLR has also been made akin to SCBs. All deposits with sponsor banks, which were earlier considered as part of the SLR, were to be converted into approved securities on maturity in order to be reckoned for the SLR purpose.

The Banking Regulation Amendment Act, 2007 has removed the floor limit of 25 percent for SLR for scheduled banks. SLR was reduced to 24 percent in November 2008 in view of the global financial crisis and the consequent need to pump additional liquidity in the market.

The second largest category of investors in the government securities market is the insurance companies. According to the stipulations of the Insurance Regulation and Development Authority of India (IRDA), all companies carrying out the business of life insurance should invest a minimum of 25 percent of their controlled funds in government securities. Similarly, companies carrying on general insurance business are required to invest 30 percent of their total assets in government securities and other guaranteed securities, of which not less than 20 percent should be in Central Government securities. For pension and general annuity business, the IRDA stipulates that 20 percent of their assets should be invested in government securities.

The non-Government provident funds, superannuation funds and gratuity funds are required by the Central Government from January 24, 2005 to invest 40 percent of their incremental accretions in Central and State government securities and/or units of gilt funds regulated by the Securities and Exchange Board of India (SEBI) and any other negotiable securities fully and unconditionally guaranteed by the Central/State Governments.

Non-banking financial companies (NBFCs) accepting public deposits are required to maintain 15 percent of such outstanding deposits in liquid assets, of which not less than 10 percent should be maintained in approved securities, including government securities and government guaranteed bonds. Investment in government securities should be in dematerialised form, which can be maintained in Constituents' Subsidiary General Ledger

(CSGL) Account of a SCB/Stock Holding Corporation of India Limited (SHCIL). In order to increase the security and liquidity of their deposits, residuary non-banking companies (RNBCs), are required to invest not less than 95 percent of their aggregate liability to depositors (ALD) as outstanding on December 31, 2005 and entire incremental deposits over this level in directed investments, which include government securities, rated and listed securities and debt oriented mutual funds. From April 1, 2007, the entire ALD is required to be invested in directed investments only.

To sum up, development of the Government securities market is critical for facilitating active public debt management policy, development and integration of financial markets and operation of indirect instruments of monetary policy. The development of the government securities market has been pursued since the early 1990s with the objectives of ensuring smooth conduct of the government's market borrowings, enlarging the investor base and facilitating the emergence of a risk-free rupee yield curve.

In India, the government securities market has witnessed significant transformation in its various dimensions, viz. market-based price discovery, widening of the investor base, introduction of new instruments, establishment of primary dealers and electronic trading and settlement infrastructure. This is the outcome of persistent and high-quality reforms in developing the government securities market. There are still areas where further development needs to be undertaken. Increased transparency and disclosures, gradual scaling down of mandated instruments and development of newer instruments are some major areas which could be considered. Regulatory incentives to increase the size of the trading book could be considered as a measure to further develop the government securities market.

Presently, investor base includes not only banks and insurance companies, but also private companies, private mutual funds, finance companies and individuals. Keeping this in view, a number of reform measures were initiated in this segment, which had a positive impact on both the primary and the secondary markets. Reforms in the government securities market have been introduced to impart liquidity and depth to the market by widening the investor base and by ensuring market-clearing interest rate mechanisms.

14

Capital Market in the Pre-reforms and Post-reforms Periods

An efficient capital market is an important constituent of a sound financial system. In India, efforts have been made in recent years to set up an effective regulatory framework covering major participants in the capital market. Similarly, the technology of trading and settlements in the stock exchanges has been upgraded. Internet-based trading in securities has been permitted. Foreign institutional investors (FIIs) and pension funds were allowed to enter the Indian stock market from 1993 onwards. The market has undergone a major transformation in terms of its structure, products, practices, spread, institutional framework and other important aspects like transparency, integrity and efficiency since then. The size of the market has also grown manifold.

14.1 Meaning and Importance of Capital Market

Capital market is a market for long-term funds. The distinction between capital market and money market is not watertight. Broadly speaking, capital market focuses on financing of fixed investment (machinery and equipment) while money market provides working capital finance (raw material etc.).

Capital market channelises household savings to the corporate sector and allocates funds to firms. In this process, it allows both firms and households to share risks associated with business. Moreover, capital market enables the valuation of firms on an almost continuous basis and plays an important role in the governance of the corporate sector.

Capital market fosters economic growth in following ways:

1. It augments the quantum of savings and capital formation in the economy.

2. It allocates capital efficiently thereby raising the productivity of investment.
3. It enhances the efficiency of a financial system as diverse competitors vie with each other for financial resources.
4. It adds to the financial deepening of the economy by enlarging the financial sector and promoting the use of innovative, sophisticated and cost-effective financial instruments, which ultimately reduce the cost of capital.
5. Well-functioning capital markets also impose discipline on firms to perform.
6. Equity and debt markets stress on the banking sector by diversifying credit risk across the economy.

14.2 Capital Market in the Pre-reforms Period (i.e. Pre-1991)

Historically, different kinds of financial intermediaries have existed in the Indian financial system. At the time of Independence in 1947, working capital requirements of corporates were financed mainly by commercial banks. As the capital market was underdeveloped, a number of development finance institutions (DFIs) were set up at the all-India and the State levels to meet the long-term fund requirements of companies.

Prior to the onset of financial sector reforms in 1991, the capital market structure in India was subject to several controls and opaque procedures. The objective of control over capital issues was to channel the limited capital resources available for investment in the country into desired areas. Apart from this main objective, capital issues control was put to several other uses, these being the following:

1. Regulation of bonus issues.
2. Regulation of terms and conditions of foreign capital participation in Indian companies and the regulation of the terms and conditions of dilution or repatriation of foreign equity.
3. Regulation of capital re-organisation plans of companies,

including mergers and amalgamations.

4. Regulation of the capital structure of companies, as well as the terms and conditions of additional issues.
5. Regulation of the volume and timing of the private issue of capital.

Moreover, the trading and settlement system was outdated and not in tune with international practices. Raising of capital from the market was regulated by the Capital Issues (Control) Act, 1947 which was administered by the Controller of Capital Issues (CCIs) in the Ministry of Finance, Government of India. The scheme of controls under the Act required all the companies to obtain prior consent for issues of capital to the public. Pricing as well as the features of the capital structure (such as debt-equity ratios), were controlled by the Government. Similarly, the Securities Contracts (Regulation) Act, 1956 was administered by the Directorate of Stock Exchanges also in the Ministry of Finance. It empowered the Government to recognise/derecognise stock exchanges, stipulate rules and by-laws for their functioning, compel listing of securities by public companies etc. Such a system of regulation and control was fragmented and inadequate in the context of liberalisation wave sweeping across the world. Urgent measures were needed to relax controls and modernise the functioning of capital market.

14.3 Capital Market in the Post-reforms Period (i.e. since 1991)

The Indian equity market has witnessed a series of reforms since the early 1990s. The reforms have been implemented in a gradual and sequential manner, based on international best practices and modified to suit the needs of the country. The reform measures were aimed at the following:

1. Creating growth-enabling institutions.
2. Boosting competitive conditions in the equity market through improved price discovery mechanism.
3. Putting in place an appropriate regulatory framework.
4. Reducing the transaction costs.

5. Reducing information asymmetry, thereby boosting the investor confidence.

These measures were expected to increase the role of the equity market in resource mobilisation by enhancing the access of corporate sector to large resources through a variety of marketable securities. Institutional development was at the core of the reform process.

Reforms in the capital market have had a multi-dimensional impact. The significance of the capital market has improved in providing a mechanism for allocation of resources as is reflected in increase in its share in the sources of finance for the corporates. Various indicators such as reduced volatility are pointers in the direction of increase in the safety of the market. The safety of the market has also been considerably enhanced by adoption of risk management practices and the setting up of settlement guarantee funds and investor protection funds. The integrity and transparency of the market has also gone up with the wider availability of information regarding the performance of corporates.

The trading and settlement framework in the Indian stock exchanges now compares favourably with the best international practices. Liquidity in the market has improved considerably.

14.4 Introduction of Free Pricing

Raising of capital from the securities market before 1992 was regulated under the Capital Issues (Control) Act, 1947. Firms were required to obtain approval from the Controller of Capital Issues (CCI) for raising resources in the market. New companies were allowed to issue shares only at par. Only the existing companies with substantial reserves could issue shares at a premium, which was based on some prescribed formula. In 1992, the Capital Issues (Control) Act, 1947 was repealed and with this ended all controls related to raising of resources from the market. Since then the issuers of securities can raise capital from the market without requiring any consent from any authority, either for making the issue or for pricing it.

Restrictions on rights and bonus issues have also been removed. New as well as established companies are now able to price their issues according to their assessment of market conditions.

However, issuers of capital are required to meet the guidelines of SEBI on disclosure and investor protection. Companies issuing capital are required to make sufficient disclosures, including justification of the issue price and also material disclosure about the risk factors in their offer prospectus. These guidelines have served as an important measure for protecting the interest of investors and promoting the development of primary market along sound lines.

It may be recalled that in the early 1990s, the liberalisation of the industrial sector and free pricing of capital issues led to an increased number of companies tapping the primary capital market to mobilise resources. Several corporates charged a high premium not justified by their fundamentals. Also, several companies vanished after raising resources from the capital market. SEBI, therefore, strengthened the norms for public issues while retaining the freedom of the issuers to enter the new issues market and to freely price their issues. The disclosure standards were also strengthened for companies coming out with public issues for improving the levels of investor protection. Strict disclosure norms and entry point restrictions prescribed by SEBI made it difficult for most new companies without an established track record to access the public issues market. Whereas this helped to improve the quality of paper coming into the market, it contributed to a decline in the number of issues and the amount mobilised from the market.

14.5 Strengthening of Disclosure Norms

The central goal of securities markets is to obtain a widely-dispersed ownership and trading in securities. There is conflict of interest between the management team, which controls the firm, and the shareholders, who run the firm. Many policy efforts in recent years have been devoted towards improving incentives to managers to maximise the interests of shareholders.

Improvements in disclosure are a central tool for containing the conflicts of interest between the managers and shareholders. In order to foster improvements in disclosure, SEBI set up a system named electronic data information filing and retrieval (EDIFAR) in July 2002. This system offers a mechanism through which firms would electronically file mandatory disclosures to SEBI, and these documents would be available to individuals over the internet, with a near-zero delay. It is envisaged that in the future, disclosure would take place through company websites, exchange websites, and EDIFAR.

For strengthening the process of information flow from the listed companies, several measures have been introduced: (a) while sufficient disclosures are mandatory for the companies at the stage of public issues, the listed companies are also required under the listing agreement to make disclosures on a continued basis, (b) for ensuring quick flow of information to the public, the decision pertaining to dividend, bonus and right announcements or any material event are now required to be disclosed to the public within 15 minutes of the conclusion of the board meeting in which the disclosures are taken, and (c) accounting practices were streamlined with norms introduced for segment reporting, related to party transactions and consolidated balance sheets.

There is a substantial scale of securities issuance taking place through the private placement route. The private placement route has become a mechanism where securities can be placed with a few wholesale buyers of securities, without incurring the overheads of the public issue. SEBI is working on devising clear institutional mechanisms through which some public disclosure is made about these issues, while preserving the rights of issuers to not use the public issue route if it is considered to involve excessive overhead costs.

Without seeking to control the freedom of the issuers to enter the market and freely price their issues, the norms for public issues were made stringent in April 1996 to prevent fraudulent companies from accessing the market. Issuers of capital are now required to disclose information on various aspects such as track record of profitability, risk factors etc. As a result, there has been an improvement in the standards of disclosure in the offer documents for the public and rights issues and easier accessibility of information to the investors. The improvement in disclosure standards has enhanced transparency, thereby improving the level of investor protection.

14.6 Transparency and Efficiency

The National Stock Exchange (NSE) introduced screen-based trading at its inception in 1992 which was followed by other stock exchanges. Screen-based trading makes online, electronic, anonymous and order-driven transactions possible. It is a transparent system which provides equal access to all investors, irrespective of their geographical locations.

The move to an electronic trading system has resulted in transparency in trades, better price discovery and lower transaction costs. The efficiency of the market has improved through faster execution of trades. The operational efficiency of the stock market has also been strengthened through improvements in the clearing and settlement practices and the risk management process. Almost the entire delivery of securities now takes place in dematerialised form. Over the past few years or so, there has been no instance of postponement or clubbing of settlements at two main stock exchanges (BSE and NSE) despite defaults by brokers. The cases of bad deliveries are close to nil. Insider trading has been made a criminal offence. Non-transparent products like *badla* have been banned.

The setting up of trade/settlement guarantee funds in most of the exchanges has considerably reduced settlement risks for investors. Corporate governance practices and disclosure norms have led to transparency in information flows, which in turn have improved the price discovery process.

In order to bring greater transparency to the debt market, and to move away from bilateral negotiation towards anonymous order-matching, trading in government bonds began on stock exchanges on January 16, 2003. This has involved exploiting the identical process flow used for trading in equities. Trade takes place by anonymous order matching for all orders across the country, risk management is done by the clearing corporation, and settlement takes place at the depository. Under this system, government bonds appear in the depository statement of an investor alongside corporate equities and bonds. This system has several strengths.

1. Anonymous trading avoids the supervisory and regulatory difficulties of the telephone market, where counterparties are aware of identities and can engage in trades at off-market prices.
2. This market design offers symmetric market access from locations all over India and over the internet, as opposed to the telephone market, which favours entities in south Bombay.
3. It exploits information technology to guarantees that orders are matched against the best price available in the country. This is in contrast with the telephone market, where traders can search for counterparties, but are not sure of having found the best counterparty.
4. It is fully transparent in that orders and trades are visible in real time. This is in contrast with the telephone market, where orders are not visible, and the transparency of trades is limited and delayed.
5. It exploits the information technology of the depositories of the equity market (NSDL and CDSL), which have the full range of functionality required for investors such as a wide network of IT-enabled depository participants, internet access, strong computer security, access to data about the beneficial owner down to the end-investor.

Issuers also have the option of raising resources through fixed price mechanism or the book building process. [1] Book building was introduced to improve the transparency in pricing of the scrips and determine proper market price for shares.

14.7 Shortening of Settlement Cycle

Capital, unlike labour, is perpetually recycled, and the shorter the cycle, the more efficient is the use of such capital.

Following the enactment of the Depository Act, 1996, two depositories were set up: Central Depository Services Ltd. (CDSL) and National Securities Depository Limited (NSDL). The CDSL and NSDL have been successful in the dematerialisation of securities almost to the full extent. Presently, the transfer of ownership is mostly done through book-entry form. This has greatly improved the speed, accuracy and security of the settlement system. Prior to these arrangements, the settlement cycle was as high as 14 days for specified scrips and 30 days for others. The settlement risk was very high because of unforeseen happenings between the transaction and the settlement. To begin with, the settlement cycle was reduced to a week. Thereafter, rolling settlement was introduced on a T+5 basis in July 2001. From December 2001, all scrips which had established connectivity with the above-mentioned Depositories were moved to rolling settlement. The settlement cycle was further reduced to T+3 in April 2002 and to T+2 in April 2003.

14.8 Growth of Service Providers

Besides strengthening the institutional design of the markets, the reforms have also brought about an increase in the number of service providers who add value to the market. The most significant development in this respect has been the setting up of credit rating agencies. By assigning ratings to debt instruments and by continuous monitoring and dissemination of the ratings, they help in improving the quality of information. At present, six credit rating agencies are operating in India. Besides, two other service providers, *viz*. registrars to issue and share transfer agents, have also grown in number, which help in spreading the services easily and at competitive prices.

14.9 Protection of Investors

14.9.1 Investor Protection Fund: The stock exchanges have put in place a system for redressal of investor grievances for matters relating to trading members and companies. They ensure that critical and price-sensitive information reaching the exchange is made available to all classes of investor at the same point of time. Further, to protect the interests of investors, the Investor Protection Fund (IPF) has also been set up by the stock exchanges. The exchanges maintain an IPF to take care of investor claims, which may arise out of non-settlement of obligations by the trading member, who has been declared a defaulter, in respect of trades executed on the exchange. Measures of investor protection that have been put in place over the reform period have led to increased confidence among investors. [2] To improve the availability of information to investors, all listed companies are required to publish unaudited financial results on a quarterly basis.

A continuing increase in the savings rate of households suggests that there is no supply constraint in terms of financial resources that could be channelled into the equity market. After the exuberance of the stock market in the mid-1990s and its decline thereafter, a large number of individual investors took flight to safety in bank deposits, safe retirement instruments and insurance. Households in India have increasingly tended to prefer savings in the form of safe and contractual instruments as opposed to capital market based instruments. Although retail investors have started showing some increased interest in the equity market in recent years, there is a need to increase their participation further.

14.9.2 Investor Protection in Derivatives Market:

A. Guiding Principles of Derivatives Market: L.C. Gupta Committee on Derivatives Trading in India recommended the following four guiding principles of derivatives market in India:

- **Fairness and Transparency:** The trading rules should ensure that trading is conducted in a fair and transparent manner. Experience in other countries shows that in many cases, derivative brokers/dealers failed to disclose potential risk to the clients. In this context, sales practices adopted by dealers for derivatives would require specific regulation. In some of the most widely reported mishaps in the derivatives market elsewhere, the underlying reason was inadequate internal control system at the user-firm itself so that overall exposure was not controlled and the use of derivatives was for speculation rather than for risk hedging. These experiences provide useful lessons for us for designing regulations.

- **Safeguard for Clients' Moneys:** Moneys and securities deposited by clients with the trading members should not only be kept in a separate clients' account but should also not be attachable for meeting the broker's own debts. It should be ensured that trading by dealers on own account is totally segregated from that for clients.
- **Competent and Honest Service:** The eligibility criteria for trading members should be designed to encourage competent and qualified personnel so that investors/clients are served well. This makes it necessary to prescribe qualification for derivatives brokers/dealers and the sales persons appointed by them in terms of a knowledge base.
- **Market Integrity:** The trading system should ensure that the market's integrity is safeguarded by minimising the possibility of defaults. This requires framing appropriate rules about capital adequacy, margins, clearing corporation etc.

B. Measures to Protect the Rights of Investors in the Derivatives Market: Investors' money has to be kept separate at all levels and is permitted to be used only against the liability of the investor and is not available to the trading member or clearing member or even any other investor.

A trading member is required to provide every investor with a risk disclosure document which will disclose the risks associated with the derivatives trading so that investors can take a conscious decision to trade in derivatives.

Investors get the contract note duly time stamped for

receipt of the order and execution of the order. The order is executed with the identity of the client and without client ID order is not accepted by the system. The investors can demand the trade confirmation slip with their respective ID in support of the contract note. This protects them from the risk of price favours, if any, extended by the Member.

In the derivatives market all money paid by the investors towards margins on all open positions is kept in trust with the clearing house/clearing corporation and in the event of default of the trading or clearing member the amounts paid by the client towards margins are segregated and not utilized towards the default of the member. However, in the event of default of a member, losses suffered by the investors, if any, on settled/closed out position are compensated from the investors' protection fund, as per the rules, by-laws and regulations of the derivative segment of the exchanges.

14.9.3 Financial Literacy: Financial literacy is the possession of a set of skills and knowledge which allow an individual to make informed and effective decisions with all of his financial resources. Understanding basic financial concepts allows people to know how to navigate in the financial system. People with appropriate financial literacy training make better financial decisions and manage money better that those without such training.

Financial literacy focuses on the ability to manage personal finance matters in an efficient manner, and it includes the knowledge of making appropriate decisions about personal finance such as investing, insurance, real estate, budgeting, retirement and tax planning. Financial literacy also involves the proficiency of financial principles and concepts such as financial planning, compound interest, managing debt, profitable savings techniques and the time value of money.

The main steps to achieving financial literacy include learning the skills to create a budget, the ability to track spending, learning the techniques to pay off debt and effectively planning for retirement. These steps can also include counselling from a financial expert. Education about the topic involves understanding how money works, creating and achieving financial goals and managing internal and external financial challenges.

There are many advantages of financial literacy. Financial literacy helps individuals to become self-sufficient so that they can achieve financial stability. Those who understand the subject should be able to answer several questions about purchases, such as whether an item is required, whether it is affordable, and whether it an asset or a liability. This skill can help a person develop a financial road map to identify what he earns, what he spends and what he owes. This topic also affects small business owners, who greatly contribute to economic growth and stability.

The lack of financial literacy can lead to owing large amounts of debt and making poor financial decisions. Similarly, financial illiteracy may lead to making poor financial choices that can have negative consequences on the financial well-being of an individual. Financial illiteracy affects all ages and all socio-economic levels. Financial illiteracy causes many people to become victims of predatory lending, sub-prime mortgages, and fraud and high interest rates, potentially resulting in bad credit, bankruptcy or foreclosure.

14.10 Issues and Concerns

The role of equity market in capital formation continues to be limited. The private corporate debt market is active mainly in the form of private placements, while the public issue market for corporate debt is yet to pick up. It is the primary equity and debt markets that link the issuers of securities and investors and provide resources for capital formation. A growing economy requires risk capital and long-term resources in the form of debt for enabling the corporates to choose an appropriate mix of debt and equity. Long-term resources are also important for financing infrastructure projects. Therefore, in order to sustain India's high growth path, the capital market needs to play a major role. The significance of a well-functioning domestic capital market has also increased as banks need to raise necessary capital from the market to sustain their growing operations.

A major issue which will influence India's securities markets in the future is the challenge of globalisation. RBI has increasingly moved in the direction of giving access to international diversification to institutional investors and individual investors in India. Financial intermediaries and exchanges in India will also experience global competition. There is a need for fully integrating a global perspective into the plans of firms, exchanges, regulators and policy makers.

The Indian capital market has become modern in terms of market infrastructure and trading and settlement practices. The capital market has also become a much safer place than it was before the reform process began. The secondary capital market in India has also become deep and liquid. There has also been a reduction in transaction costs and significant improvement in efficiency and transparency. However, the role of the domestic capital market in capital formation in the country, both directly and indirectly through mutual funds, continues to be less significant.

Post-liberalization, the Indian stock market witnessed a number of scams due to which small investors are reluctant to enter the market. History has witnessed how regulators remained mute spectators, allowing brokers to trap investors. If the government wants investors back in the capital market, it needs to strengthen the regulators, make them efficient, accountable and investor-friendly. In the current scenario of volatile stock market, which is now a fact of life in the globalised economy, investors have to be on their toes and take proactive decisions. They cannot be docile investors, either be active or be out of business. They should not take the market as a place for speculators and punters. In civilized societies, the law and legal system are supposed to protect the interests of those who lend and not those who fail to repay.

To sum up, the capital market has been an important source

of funding for larger companies and the opening of the economy to portfolio flows from foreign institutional investors (FIIs). In recent years, companies have raised significant funds through new issues.

However, this mechanism has been used mainly by the larger companies to raise funds. There are no effective institutions that can channel equity funding to smaller companies and start-ups. In a knowledge economy, there is need to encourage the growth of venture capital funds and angel investors.

Endnotes

1. Book-building is a process by which demand for the securities proposed to be issued is built-up and the price for securities is assessed for determination of the quantum of such securities to be issued.
2. The World Bank in its survey of *Doing Business* has worked out an investor protection index, which measures the strength of minority shareholders against directors' misuse of corporate assets for his/ her personal gain. The index is the average of the disclosure index, director liability index, and shareholder suits index. The index ranges from 1 to 10, with higher values indicating better investor protection. Based on this index, India fares better than a large number of economies, including even some of the developed ones such as France and Germany.

15

Corporate Debt Market

The stock markets in India have become modern and are comparable to the best in the world in terms of market infrastructure, trading and settlement practices and risk management systems. However, given the size of the Indian economy, the capital raised from the securities market has remained quite small. Corporates, by and large, tend to finance their investment activities through alternative sources, which have inhibited the growth of the market. Large and well-known corporates in India have tended to prefer international capital markets. Huge resources have also been raised by way of debt issues from the private placement market, which is less cumbersome, fast and economical. However, this segment lacks transparency and appears to be growing at the expense of the public issues segment. Lack of sufficient capital market activity has hindered the process of diversification of investment from fixed income instruments to equity-based instruments by the households.

15.1 Significance of the Corporate Debt Market

There are many reasons why bond markets are important for an emerging economy. Prominent among these is the fact that they lead to more efficient entrepreneurship and greater value creation. When an entrepreneur takes a loan or issues bonds, all additional profit over and above the pre-fixed repayment amount accrues to the entrepreneur. So he or she is better incentivized to take sharper decisions. By having a weak bond market, this efficiency is lost. Further, this efficiency gap may well mean that there is less lending and hence less investment and entrepreneurship in the economy than is feasible.

In any country, companies face different types of financing choices at different stages of development. Reflecting the varied supplies of different types of capital and their costs, regulatory policies and financial innovations, the financing patterns of firms vary geographically and temporally. While developed countries rely more on market-based sources of finance, the developing countries rely more on bank-based sources. The development of a corporate bond market, for direct financing of the capital requirements of corporates by investors assumes paramount importance, particularly in a liberalised financial system.

Corporate debt market provides an alternative means of long-term resources to corporates—alternative to financing by banks and financial institutions. The size and growth of private corporate debt market depends upon several factors, including financing patterns of companies. Among market-based sources of financing, while the equity markets have been largely developed, the corporate bond markets in most developing countries have remained relatively underdeveloped. This has been the result of dominance of the banking system combined with the weaknesses in market infrastructure and inherent complexities.

However, credit squeeze following the Asian financial crisis in the mid-1990s drew attention of policy makers to the importance of multiple financing channels in an economy. Alternative sources of finance, apart from banks, need to be actively developed to support higher levels of investment and economic growth. The development of corporate debt market has, therefore, become the prime concern of regulators in developing countries.

From the perspective of developing countries, a liquid corporate bond market can play a critical role in supporting economic development in the following ways:

1. It supplements the banking system to meet the requirements of the corporate sector for long-term capital investment and asset creation.

2. It provides a stable source of finance when the equity market is volatile.
3. With the decline in the role of specialised financial institutions, there is an increasing realisation of the need for a well-developed corporate debt market as an alternative source of finance.
4. Corporate bond markets can also help firms reduce their overall cost of capital by allowing them to tailor their asset and liability profiles to reduce the risk of maturity and currency mismatches.
5. Corporate bond market is important for nurturing a credit culture and market discipline.
6. The existence of a well-functioning bond market can lead to the efficient pricing of credit risk as expectations of all bond market participants are incorporated into bond prices.

Apart from providing a channel for financing investments, the corporate bond markets also contribute towards portfolio diversification for holders of long-term funds. Effective asset management requires a balance of asset alternatives. In view of the underdeveloped state of the corporate bond markets, there would be an overweight position in government securities and even equities. The existence of a well-functioning corporate bond market widens the array of asset choices for long-term investors such as pension funds and insurance companies and allows them to better manage the maturity structure of their balance sheets.

15.2 Lessons from East Asian Crisis

In many Asian economies, banks have traditionally been performing the role of financial intermediation. The East Asian crisis of 1997 underscored the limitations of weak banking systems. The primary role of a banking system is to create and maintain liquidity that is needed to finance production within a short-term horizon. The crisis showed that over-reliance on bank lending for debt financing exposes an economy to the risk of a failure of the banking system. Banking systems, therefore, cannot be the sole source of long-term investment capital without making an economy vulnerable to external shocks. In times of financial distress, when banking sector becomes vulnerable, the corporate bond markets act as a buffer and reduce macroeconomic vulnerability to shocks and systemic risk through diversification of credit and investment risks. By contributing to a more diverse financial system, a bond market can promote financial stability. A bond market may also help the banking system in difficult conditions by allowing banks to recapitalise their balance sheets through securitisation.

Presently, when India is endeavouring to sustain its high growth rate, it is necessary that financing constraints in any form are removed and alternative financing channels are developed in a systematic manner for supplementing traditional bank credit. The problem of *missing* corporate bond market, however, is not unique to India alone. Predominantly bank-dominated financial systems in most Asian economies faced this situation. Many Asian economies woke up to meet this challenge in the wake of the Asian financial crisis. During less than a decade, the domestic bond markets of many Asian economies have undergone significant transformation. In the case of India, however, the small size of the private corporate debt market has shrunk further. This trend needs to be reversed soon. India could learn from the experiences of countries that have undertaken the process of reforming their domestic corporate bond markets.

15.3 Corporate Debt Market in India

India is now one of the fastest growing economies in the world and is endeavouring to step up the growth rate. Limited availability of adequate long-term resources could adversely affect India's infrastructure development. Infrastructure financing requirements are large and could not be expected to be met by the banking sector alone. Banks already appear to have significant exposure to long-term funds. They may, therefore, not be in a position to fund long-term projects in future to the extent they have been able to do in recent years. Inadequate long-term resources could, therefore, act as a constraint on India's future growth prospects.

In the absence of a well-functioning debt market, even large corporates fund their requirements from the banking system, limiting the availability of bank funds for small and medium enterprises and other sectors. This also raises the cost of borrowings for them. Thus, development of the capital market, in general, and the debt market, in particular, is crucial from the point of view of reducing corporate sector's reliance on the banking system so as to enable it to focus more on lending to small and medium enterprises, and agriculture and allied activities.

Corporates in India have traditionally relied heavily on borrowings from banks and financial institutions (FIs) to finance their investments. Equity financing has also been used, but largely during periods of surging equity prices. However, bond issuances by companies have remained limited in size and scope. Given the huge funding requirements, especially for long-term infrastructure projects, the corporate debt market has a crucial role to play and needs to be nurtured.

In India, banks and FIs have traditionally been the most important external sources of finance for the corporate sector. The second half of the 1980s saw some activity in primary bond issuances, but these were largely by the public sector undertakings (PSUs). The corporates relied more on banks for meeting short-term working capital requirements and DFIs for financing long-term investment. However, in view of the declining role of DFIs in recent years, a gap has appeared for long-term finance. Commercial banks have managed to fill this gap, but only to an extent as there are asset-liability mismatch issues for banks in providing longer-maturity credit.

In the 1990s, the equity market in India witnessed a series of reforms, which helped in bringing it on par with international standards. However, the corporate debt market has not been able to develop due to lack of market infrastructure and a comprehensive regulatory framework. For a variety of reasons, the issuers resorted to private placement of bonds as opposed to public issues of bonds.

15.3.1 Emergence of Private Placement Market: In private placement, resources are raised privately through arrangers (merchant banking intermediaries) who place securities with a limited number of investors such as financial institutions, corporates and high net worth individuals. Under Section 81 of the Companies Act, 1956, a private placement is defined as 'an issue of shares or of convertible securities by a company to a select group of persons'. An offer of securities to more than 50 persons is deemed to be a public issue under the Act. Corporates access the private placement market because of its following advantages:

1. It is a cost and time-effective method of raising funds.
2. It can be structured to meet the needs of the entrepreneurs.

Private placement does not require detailed compliance of formalities as required in public or rights issues.

The emergence of private placement market has provided an easier alternative to the corporates to raise funds. Although the private placement market provides a cost-effective and time-saving mechanism for raising resources, the unbridled growth of this market has raised some concerns. The quality of issues and extent of transparency in the private placement deals remain areas of concern even though privately placed issues by listed companies are now required to be listed and also subject to necessary disclosures. In the case of public issues, all the issues coming to the market are screened for their quality and the investors rely on ratings and other public information for evaluation of risk.

Such a screening mechanism is missing in the case of private placements. This increases the risk associated with privately placed securities. Further, the private placement market appears to be growing at the expense of the public issues market, which has some distinct advantages in the form of wider participation by the investors and, thus, diversification of the risk.

The private placement market was not regulated until May 2004. In view of the mushrooming growth of the market and the risk posed by it, SEBI prescribed that the listing of all debt securities, irrespective of the mode of issuance, i.e. whether issued on a private placement basis or through public/rights issue, shall be done through a separate listing agreement. The RBI also issued guidelines to the financial intermediaries under its purview on investments in non-SLR securities, including private placement.

In June 2001, boards of banks were advised to lay down policy and prudential limits on investments in bonds and debentures, including cap on unrated issues and on a private placement basis. The policy laid down by banks should prescribe stringent appraisal of issues, especially by non-borrower customers, provide for an internal system of rating, stipulate entry-level minimum ratings/quality standards and put in place proper risk management systems.

15.3.2 Credit Default Swaps (CDS) for Corporate Bonds: The objective of introducing CDS for corporate bonds is to provide market participants a tool to transfer and manage credit risk in an effective manner through redistribution of risk. CDS, as a risk management product, offers the participants the opportunity to hive off credit risk and also to assume credit risk which otherwise may not be possible. Since CDS have benefits like enhancing investment and borrowing opportunities and reducing transaction costs while allowing risk transfers, such a product would increase investors' interest in corporate bonds and would be beneficial to the development of the corporate bond market in India.

Guidelines on CDS for corporate bonds were issued by the RBI on May 23, 2011, outlining broad norms including the eligible participants and other requirements. It was also indicated that market participants would have to follow the capital adequacy guidelines for CDS issued by their respective regulators. Subsequently, guidelines were issued stating that NBFCs shall participate in CDS market only as users. As users, they are permitted to buy credit protection only to hedge their credit risk on the corporate bonds they hold. They are not permitted to sell protection and hence not permitted to enter into short positions in the CDS contracts. However, they are permitted to exit their bought CDS positions by unwinding them with the original counterparty or by assigning them in favour of the buyer of the underlying bond.

15.4 Reasons for Slow Growth of Corporate Debt Market

Development of the domestic corporate debt market in India is constrained by a number of factors as listed below:

1. Low issuance leading to illiquidity in the secondary market.
2. Narrow investor base.
3. Inadequate credit assessment skills.
4. High costs of issuance.
5. Lack of transparency in trades.
6. Non-standardised instruments.
7. Comprehensive regulatory framework.
8. Underdevelopment of securitisation products.

The market suffers from deficiencies in products, participants and institutional framework. This is despite the fact that India is fairly well-placed insofar as pre-requisites for the development of the corporate bond market are concerned.

There is a reasonably well-developed government securities market, which generally precedes the development of the market for corporate debt securities. The major stock exchanges have trading platforms for the transactions in debt securities. The infrastructure also exists for clearing and settlement. The Clearing Corporation of India Limited (CCIL) has been successfully settling trades in government bonds, foreign exchange and other money market instruments. The experience with the depository system has been satisfactory. The presence of multiple rating agencies meets the requirement of an assessment framework for bond quality.

15.5 High Level Expert Committee on Corporate Debt and Securitisation

With the intent of the development of the corporate bond market along sound lines, some initiatives have been taken by the SEBI in the past few years. These measures have largely aimed at improving disclosures in respect of privately placed debt issues. In view of the immediate need to design a suitable framework for the corporate debt market, the Union Budget 2005-06 announced the setting up of a High Level Expert Committee on Corporate Bonds and Securitisation to look into the legal, regulatory, tax and mortgage design issues for the development of the corporate bond market. The High Level Committee (Chairman: R.H. Patil), which submitted its report in December 2005, looked into the factors inhibiting the development of an active corporate debt market in India and made several suggestions for developing the market infrastructure for development of primary as well as secondary corporate bond market.

The key recommendations of the Committee are summed up below.

15.5.1 Corporate Debt Market:

A. Primary Market

1. The stamp duty on debt instruments be made uniform across all the States and linked to the tenor of securities.
2. To increase the issuer base, the time and cost for public issuance and the disclosure and listing requirements for private placements be reduced and made simpler. Banks be allowed to issue bonds of maturities of 5 year and above for ALM purpose, in addition to infrastructure sector bonds.
3. A suitable framework for market making be put in place.
4. Disclosure requirements be substantially abridged for listed companies. For unlisted companies, rating rationale should form the basis of listing. Companies that wish to make a public issue should be subjected to stringent disclosure requirements. The privately placed bonds

should be listed within 7 days from the date of allotment, as in the case of public issues.

5. Role of debenture trustees should be strengthened. SEBI should encourage development of professional debenture trustee companies.
6. To reduce the relative cost of participation in the corporate bond market, the tax deduction at source (TDS) rule for corporate bonds should be brought at par with the government securities. Companies should pay interest and redemption amounts to the depository, which would then pass them on to the investors through ECS/warrants.
7. For widening investor base, the scope of investment by provident/pension/gratuity funds and insurance companies in corporate bonds should be enhanced. Retail investors should be encouraged to participate in the market through stock exchanges and mutual funds.
8. To create large floating stocks, the number of fresh issuances by a given corporate in a given time period should be limited. Any new issue should preferably be a reissue so that there are large stocks in any given issue and issuers should be encouraged to consolidate various existing issues into a few large issues, which can then serve as benchmarks.
9. A centralised database of all bonds issued by corporates be created. Enabling regulations for setting up platforms for non-competitive bidding and electronic bidding process for primary issuance of bonds should be created.

B. Secondary Market

1. Regulatory framework for a transparent and efficient secondary market for corporate bonds should be put in place by SEBI in a phased manner. To begin with, a trade reporting system for capturing information related to trading in corporate bonds and disseminating on a real time basis should be created. The market participants should report details of each transaction within a specified time period to the trade reporting system.
2. Clearing and settlement of trades should meet the

standards set by IOSCO and global best practices. The clearing and settlement system should migrate within a reasonable timeframe from gross settlement to net settlement. The clearing and settlement agencies should be given access to the RTGS system. For improving secondary market trading, repos in corporate bonds be allowed.

3. An online order matching platform for corporate bonds should be set up by the stock exchanges or jointly by regulated institutions such as banks, financial institutions, mutual funds, insurance companies etc. In the final stage of development, the trade reporting system could migrate to STP-enabled order matching system and net settlement.
4. The Committee also recommended: (a) reduction in shut period for corporate bonds; (b) application of uniform coupon conventions such as, 30/360 day count convention as followed for government securities; (c) reduction in minimum market lot from ₹ 10 lakh to ₹ 1 lakh, and (d) introduction of exchange traded interest rate derivative products.

15.5.2 Securitised Debt Market:

1. A consensus should evolve on the affordable rates and levels of stamp duty on debt assignment, pass-through certificates (PTCs) and security receipts (SRs) across States.
2. An explicit tax pass-through treatment to securitisation SPVs/Trust SPVs should be provided. Wholesale investors should be permitted to invest in and hold units of a close-ended passively managed mutual fund whose sole objective is to invest its funds in securitised paper. There should be no withholding tax on interest paid by the borrowers to the securitisation trust and on distributions made by the securitisation trust to its PTCs and/or SR holders.
3. PTCs and other securities issued by securitisation SPVs/Trust SPVs should be notified as securities under SCRA.
4. Large-sized NBFCs and non-NBFCs corporate bodies

established in India may be permitted to invest in SRs as QIBs. Private equity funds registered with SEBI as venture capital funds (VCFs) may also be permitted to invest in SRs within the limits that are applied for investment by VCFs into corporate bonds.

5. The Committee also recommended: (a) introduction of credit enhancement mechanism for corporate bonds, (b) creation of specialised debt funds to cater to the needs of the infrastructure sector, and (c) fiscal support, like tax benefits, bond insurance and credit enhancement, for municipal bonds and infrastructure SPVs.

Learning from the experience of developing the government securities market, the development of the corporate debt market needs to proceed in a measured manner with well thought out sequencing. Such development also requires cooperation of and coordination with the key players. The initial steps towards developing the corporate bond market based on the recommendations of the High Level Expert Committee on Corporate Bonds and Securitisation have already been initiated. The Union Budget for 2006-07 had proposed to create a single unified exchange-traded market for corporate bonds. As a first step towards creation of a Unified Exchange Traded Bond Market, the SEBI has initiated steps to establish a system to capture all information related to trading in corporate bonds as accurately and as close to execution as possible through an authorised reporting platform.

The market development process for bonds in India is likely to be a gradual process as has been experienced in other countries. For step by step development of the corporate bond market, it is necessary to lay down the broad objectives, which may include: (a) building a liquid government securities benchmark yield curve for appropriate pricing of debt instruments, (b) promoting the growth of an active secondary market for spot and derivative transactions, and (c) providing encouragement to issuers and investors to participate in the bond market. All these objectives are mutually reinforcing.

To sum up, the development of any market requires removal of bottlenecks on supply as well as demand side, while putting in place alongside sound institutional and legal framework. In India, high economic growth has created ample demand for funds from the corporate sector which is reflected in sharp growth in bank credit and increased resource mobilisation from the international equity market and the private placement market. Encouraging business outlook and congenial investment climate have created stimulus for companies to undertake capacity expansion. On the supply side too, rising income levels and savings would require alternative investment options, including equity and corporate debt. The need, therefore, is to ensure that the capital market is well positioned to take advantage of these favourable factors.

There is a need to ensure that the corporates are able to raise resources from the capital market in a timely and cost-effective manner. The need is also felt to develop strong domestic institutional investors, which would serve many purposes. As the market evolution is an ongoing process, the Indian equity market would have to continuously strive to keep up to the international standards. In particular, corporate governance practices need to be strengthened further to raise the confidence level of a common investor. This would also enhance flow of institutional money to equities.

The corporate debt market is not yet large enough to have a significant impact on systemic stability. The Indian financial system is dominated by bank intermediation. Corporates in India have traditionally relied on borrowings from banks and financial institutions. Equity financing has also been used during periods of surging equity prices. The corporate bond market, which was reasonably vibrant in the mid-1980s, has however shrunk with respect to its alternate sources of funding. The lack of buying interest, low transparency and absence of pricing of spreads against the benchmark are some of the other reasons. The opening up of the capital account could, however, see the growth of the corporate bond market as there may be demand from foreign investors seeking exposure to high-quality corporate debt.

Even on the supply side, the need for the corporate bond market by the corporates is inadequate. This is due to their increased access to the off-shore market and improving off-shore spreads/risk perception resulting in greater liquidity off-shore rather than on-shore. Further, a sizable market is captured by the large issuance of credit risk-free government securities and issuance of low-risk subordinated debts at attractive interest rates by banks as part of their Tier II capital. While SEBI has initiated steps to simplify issuance procedures and reduce the costs of public issuance, the relative ease in raising corporate debt through private placements has resulted in the large share of private placement issuance of corporate bonds. This has rendered the corporate bond market relatively less transparent which has, in turn, impacted the liquidity of such bonds.

The secondary market in corporate bonds is limited to highly rated securities (AA and above). The wholesale debt segments of the stock exchanges have not picked up and the OTC market in corporate bonds lacks an automated order matching system and centralised settlement. The absence of DVP is another obstacle in market development. The tax deducted at source (TDS) system for corporate bonds acts as an impediment to the development of secondary market activities, especially since government securities are not subject to TDS. The delay in contract enforcement also hampers market development.

The development of the corporate bond market currently suffers from a lack of buying interest, absence of pricing of spreads against the benchmark and a flat yield curve. It requires regulatory and legislative reforms for its development.

16

Foreign Exchange Market

Foreign exchange market structure in India has undergone substantial transformation from the early 1990s. The market participants have become diversified and there are several instruments available to manage their risks. Sources of supply and demand in the foreign exchange market have also changed in line with the shifts in the relative importance in balance of payments from current to capital account. There has also been considerable improvement in the market infrastructure in terms of trading platforms and settlement mechanisms. Trading in Indian foreign exchange market is largely concentrated in the spot segment even as volumes in the derivatives segment are on the rise.

16.1 Pre-Independence Period

Prior to Independence in 1947, India's forex market lacked depth and liquidity. Exchange control and the fixed exchange rate regime came in the way of forex market development. Exchange control was introduced in India on September 3, 1939 following the outbreak of the Second World War, mainly to conserve the non-sterling area currencies and utilise them for essential purposes. The objective of exchange control was primarily to regulate the demand for foreign exchange for various purposes, within the limits set by the available supply. It, thus, involved rationing of foreign exchange among various competing demands for it. In the closing stages of the War, it became clear that control over foreign exchange transactions would have to continue in the post-War period in the interest of making the most prudent use of the foreign exchange resources. It was, therefore, decided to place the control on a statutory basis and the Foreign Exchange Regulation Act of

1947 was accordingly enacted. The Act came into force on March 25, 1947.

16.2 Pre-reforms Period (1947-90)

Foreign exchange market was highly regulated prior to 1991. In view of the scarcity of foreign exchange reserves, banks, exporters and individuals had to surrender the foreign exchange earned/received by them to the RBI.

In the early 1990s, the foreign exchange market in India was in the initial stages of development and suffered from several shortcomings. The spot as well as forward markets lacked depth and liquidity. The market was skewed with a handful of public sector banks accounting for bulk of the merchant business and the foreign banks a greater share of inter-bank business. The forward rates reflected demand and supply, rather than interest rate differentials due to absence of integration between the money and forex markets and the restrictions placed on borrowing/lending in the international market. On account of ceilings on open positions and gaps, there was a virtual absence of market making.

The cross-currency market had not developed on account of prohibition on initiating transactions in the overseas market. Besides forward contracts and cross currency options, there was no free access to other hedging products.

It was, therefore, felt that any attempt at vitalising the foreign exchange market should necessarily start with relaxation of regulations governing these issues.

16.3 Post-reforms Period (1991 onward)

Post-reforms period has been marked by wide-ranging measures to widen and deepen the market, besides exchange rate liberalisation. The impetus for forex market reform was provided by recommendations of the: (a) High Level Committee on Balance of Payments (Chairman: C. Rangarajan), 1993; (b) Expert Group on Foreign Exchange Markets in India (Chairman: O.P. Sodhani), 1995, and (c) Committee on Capital Account

Convertibility (Chairman: S.S. Tarapore), 1997.

16.3.1 Expert Group on Foreign Exchange Markets: The reform phase began with the Sodhani Committee (1994) which in its report submitted in 1995 made several recommendations to relax the regulations with a view to vitalising the foreign exchange market. Most of the recommendations of the Sodhani Committee relating to the development of the foreign exchange market were implemented during the latter half of the 1990s.

The Expert Group on Foreign Exchange Markets in India (Chairman: O.P. Sodhani), which submitted its Report in 1995, identified various regulations inhibiting the growth of the market. The Group's main recommendations were as follows:

1. Corporates may be permitted to take a hedge upon declaring the existence of an exposure.
2. Banks should be permitted to fix their own exchange position limits such as intra-day and overnight limits, subject to ensuring that the capital is provided/earmarked to the extent of 5 percent of this limit based on internationally accepted guidelines.
3. Fixation of Aggregate Gap Limit (AGL)—which would also include rupee transactions—by the managements of the banks based on capital, risk taking capacity etc.
4. Banks be allowed to initiate cross currency positions abroad and to lend or borrow short-term funds up to 6 months, subject to a specified ceiling.
5. Allowing exporters to retain 100 percent of their export earnings in any foreign currency with an authorised dealer (AD) in India, subject to liquidation of outstanding advances against export bills.
6. Permitting ADs to determine the interest rates and maturity period in respect of FCNR(B) deposits.
7. Selective intervention by the RBI in the market so as to ensure greater orderliness in the market.

In pursuance of the recommendations of the Sodhani Committee, the RBI had set up the Clearing Corporation of India Ltd. (CCIL) in 2001 to mitigate risks in the Indian financial markets. The CCIL commenced settlement of foreign exchange operations for inter-bank USD-INR spot and forward trades from November 8, 2002 and for inter-bank USD-INR cash and tom trades from February 5, 2004. The CCIL undertakes settlement of foreign exchange trades on a multilateral net basis through a process of novation and all spot, cash and tom transactions are guaranteed for settlement from the trade date. Every eligible foreign exchange contract entered between members gets novated or replaced by two new contracts—between the CCIL and each of the two parties, respectively.

Following the multilateral netting procedure, the net amount payable to, or receivable from, the CCIL in each currency is arrived at, member-wise. The Rupee leg is settled through the members' current accounts with the RBI and the USD leg through CCIL's account with the settlement bank at New York. The CCIL sets limits for each member bank on the basis of certain parameters such as member's credit rating, net worth, asset value and management quality. The CCIL has consistently endeavoured to add value to the services and has gradually brought the entire gamut of foreign exchange transactions under its purview. Intermediation, by the CCIL thus, provides its members the benefits of risk mitigation, improved efficiency, lower operational cost and easier reconciliation of accounts with correspondents.

16.3.2 Technical Group on Foreign Exchange Market, 2005: In order to review comprehensively the initiatives taken by the RBI from time to time in the foreign exchange market and to identify areas for further improvement, the RBI constituted an internal Technical Group. The Group, which submitted its Report in June 2005, reviewed foreign market liberalisation in select emerging markets and examined the current regulatory regime in the light of liberalisation in related sections to identify areas for further liberalisation. The Group noted that although the external sector is fundamentally stronger and more resilient than ever before, some of the preconditions for further liberalisation laid down by the Tarapore Committee on Capital Account Convertibility were yet to be achieved.

In order to embark upon further deregulation of the foreign exchange market, including relaxation of the remaining capital controls, an enabling environment was needed for the reforms to proceed on a sustainable basis. In this context, liberalisation of various sectors of the economy had to proceed in tandem to derive synergies of the reform process. The Group also took into account the risks associated with internationalisation of the rupee and concluded that a gradual and need-based approach would be more suited to the prevailing conditions.

The Group proposed various measures for implementation in the short-term for resident entities, banks and non-residents. Some of the important recommendations made by the Group are as under.

A. Resident Entities:

1. In order to provide greater flexibility to resident entities for dynamically managing their exposures, to further the development of the forward segment of the market and to bring about uniformity with respect to booking of such contracts, all forward contracts booked by residents, regardless of tenor, may be allowed to be cancelled and rebooked freely.
2. Foreign currency-rupee swaps booked to hedge genuine foreign currency exposures may also be permitted to be rebooked/reinstated on cancellation.
3. Corporates with derived foreign exchange exposures arising out of rupee-foreign currency swaps may be permitted to hedge the interest rate risk and cross currency exposures (not involving the rupee).
4. Corporates may be permitted to sell/write covered call and put options subject to adequate accounting standards and risk management systems being in place.

B. Commercial Banks:

1. Banks would be required to put in place a customer

suitability and appropriateness policy.

2. Banks may be permitted to provide capital on the actual overnight open exchange position maintained by them, rather than on their open position limits.
3. Banks may be given the freedom to decide on the period of crystallisation of unpaid export bills; the exchange gain and loss on crystallisation may be passed on to exporters symmetrically.
4. Banks having expertise in managing commodity price risk and hence specifically authorised by the RBI in this regard may be allowed to approve commodity hedging proposals from their corporate customers.
5. The closing time for inter-bank foreign exchange market in India may be extended by one hour from 4.00 p.m. to 5.00 p.m.
6. Forex data, including traded volumes for derivatives such as foreign currency-rupee options may be made available to the market on a regular basis.

C. Non-Resident Entities:

1. The Group was of the view that as at present apart from US dollar (US$), Pound sterling (GBP), Euro and Japanese yen (JPY), Foreign Currency Non-Resident (FCNR)(B) deposits may also be accepted in Canadian dollar (CAD), Australian dollar (AUD) and New Zealand dollar (NZD).

Based on the recommendations of the Technical Group, the Annual Policy Statement of the RBI for the year 2005-06 initiated several measures.

First, cancellation and rebooking of all eligible forward contracts booked by residents, irrespective of tenor, were permitted. Second, in order to guard against international price fluctuations in tradables, banks were allowed to approve proposals for commodity hedging in international exchanges from their corporate customers. Third, the closing time for inter-bank foreign exchange market in India was extended by one hour up to 5.00 p.m. Fourth, it was proposed to disseminate additional information, including traded volumes for derivatives such as foreign currency-rupee options to the market.

With a view to further liberalising the norms for raising resources abroad as also ensuring better effective use of foreign exchange reserves, it was decided to raise the ceiling of overseas investment by Indian entities in overseas joint ventures and/or wholly-owned subsidiaries from 100 percent to 200 percent of their net worth under the automatic route. Concurrently, in order to further liberalise the procedure, the authorised dealers (ADs) were accorded general permission to open foreign currency accounts of the project offices set up in India by foreign companies and operate the accounts flexibly. Earlier, ADs were required to obtain approval of the RBI.

16.4 Measures Undertaken to Develop Foreign Exchange Market

The Indian foreign exchange market has come a long way since the period prior to 1978 when banks were required to maintain square position at all points of time. The important measures undertaken to broaden and deepen the foreign exchange market are as follows:

16.4.1 General Measures:

- **March 1992:** The exchange rate of rupees was partially floated in March 1992 with the introduction of LERMS.
- **March 1993:** Unified exchange rate was introduced.
- **August 1993:** Direct quotation system was introduced.
- **July 1995:** In order to ensure that the exchange rate of the rupee reflected fully the demand supply situation and in furtherance of the move towards eliminating transactions through reserves, it was decided to route government debt service payment (civil) through the market.
- **October 1995:** With a view to minimising the influence on the process of rate formation, the Reserve Bank discontinued quoting its buying and selling rate.

16.4.2 Relaxation for Banks:

- **September 1995:** As against overnight limit of ₹ 15 crore, banks were given freedom to fix their own open exchange position limit and apply to the Reserve Bank for approval. The revised limits became operative from January 1996.

- **April 1996:** Depending upon the asset liability profile, dealing expertise and such other relevant factors, the ADs were accorded freedom to fix their own gap limits for more efficient management of their assets and liabilities subject to the Reserve Bank approval. The banks which are permitted higher limits should be in a position to mark to market their gaps on a daily basis using value at risk models.
- **April 1996:** The banks which had put in place adequate risk management systems were permitted to freely trade in the overseas markets, subject to the overall position/gap discipline.
- **October 1996:** Banks were permitted to provide foreign currency denominated loans to their customers out of the pool of FCNR(B) deposits.
- **April 1997:** Cash reserve requirements on inter-bank borrowings were removed.
- **April 1997:** The Reserve Bank permitted banks to borrow and invest in the overseas markets. Banks are permitted to borrow up to 25 percent of Tier I capital and invest up to any amount.

16.4.3 Relaxation for Corporates:

- **April 1992:** EEFC scheme was introduced. Currently, exchange earners in select categories are permitted to retain 100 percent of foreign exchange receipts in foreign currency accounts, while all others are permitted to retain 50 percent.
- **September 1996:** Corporates were accorded greater freedom to undertake active hedging. They were given freedom to choose the currency of hedge irrespective of the currency of the exposure.
- **September 1996:** Corporates were given complete freedom to book and cancel cross currency options.

Besides, several measures have been undertaken to

develop the forward market. The participants in the forward market have increased considerably. Several instruments have been introduced to hedge exposures.

16.5 Hedging for Foreign Currency Exposure

16.5.1 Hedging Facilities for Residents:

- **March 1992:** Residents in India were permitted to enter into a forward contract with an authorised dealer (AD) to hedge an exposure to exchange risk in respect of a transaction for which sale and/or purchase of foreign exchange is permitted subject to certain terms and conditions. Currently, forward contracts booked in respect of foreign currency exposures of residents falling due within one year may be freely cancelled and rebooked, among other stipulations.
- **September 1996:** Residents in India were permitted to enter into a foreign currency option contract with an AD in India to hedge foreign exchange exposure arising out of his trade, provided that in respect of cost effective risk reduction strategies like range forwards and ratio-range forwards, there is no net inflow of premium. Cross currency options should be written on a fully covered back-to-back basis. At present, the cover transaction may be undertaken with a bank outside India, an off-shore banking unit situated in a Special Economic Zone or an internationally recognised option exchange or another AD in India.
- **April 1997:** Residents who owe a foreign exchange or rupee liability, may enter into a contract for foreign currency-rupee swap with an AD in India to hedge long term exposure under certain terms and conditions.
- **October 1997:** Residents who have borrowed foreign exchange were permitted to enter into an interest rate swap or currency swap or coupon swap or foreign currency option or interest rate cap or collar (purchases) or forward rate agreement (FRA) contract with an AD in India or with

a branch outside India of an AD for hedging loan exposure and unwinding from such hedges. The contract, however, should not involve the rupee and maturity of the hedge should not exceed the unexpired maturity of the underlying loan besides other conditions.

- **September 1998:** Residents in India, engaged in import and export trade, may hedge the price risk of all commodities except crude oil and petroleum products. Hedging of price risk on these products was also permitted with effect from September 2000 in the international commodity exchanges/ markets.
- **April 2003:** ADs were permitted to enter into forward contracts with residents in respect of transactions denominated in foreign currency but settled in Indian rupees. These contracts shall be held till maturity and cash settlement would be made on the maturity date by cancellation of the contracts.
- **July 2003:** Foreign currency-rupee options were introduced. ADs were permitted to offer the product on back to back basis or run an option book as per the specified terms and conditions.
- **December 2003:** Residents having overseas direct investments were permitted to hedge the exposure under certain terms and conditions.

16.5.2 Hedging Facilities for Authorised Dealers (ADs):

- **January 1997:** ADs were permitted to use certain instruments like interest rate swaps, currency swaps, and forward rate agreements to hedge their assets-liability portfolio based on appropriate policy as approved by their top management.
- **April 1997:** A beginning for rupee based derivatives was made in India and banks were permitted to offer dollar-rupee swaps to corporates to actively manage their foreign exchange exposures. Currently no limits are placed on the ADs for undertaking swaps to facilitate corporates to hedge their foreign exchange exposures; a limit of US$ 50

million per AD is, however, fixed for net supply in the market on account of swaps enabling corporates to move from rupee to foreign currency liability.

- **October 1999:** ADs may also purchase call or put options to hedge their cross currency proprietary trading positions. The value and maturity of the hedge should not exceed that of the underlying instrument.
- **October 2002:** Authorised banks were permitted to enter into forward contracts with their constituents (exporters of gold products, jewellery manufacturers, trading houses, *etc.*) in respect of the underlying sale, purchase and loan transactions in gold.
- **November 2002:** Banks, which are allowed to enter into forward gold contracts in India were allowed to cover their price risk by hedging abroad in a similar manner.
- **November 2002:** Foreign banks were allowed to hedge the entire Tier I capital held by them in Indian books. The capital funds should be available in India to meet local regulatory and CRAR requirements. The forward contract should be for tenor of one year or more and may be rolled over on maturity. Foreign banks were permitted to hedge their Tier II capital in the form of Head Office borrowing as subordinated debt, by keeping it swapped into Indian rupees at all times.

16.5.3 Hedging Facilities for Non-Residents:

- **October 1997:** ADs were allowed to enter into forward/option contracts with NRIs to hedge: (i) the amount of dividend due on shares held in an Indian company; (ii) the amount of investment made under portfolio scheme in accordance with the relevant provisions for the purpose; and (iii) the balances held in the Foreign Currency Non-Resident (FCNR) account or the Non-Resident External Rupee (NRE) account.
- **November 2002:** Earlier, designated branches of ADs maintaining accounts of FIIs could provide forward cover under certain terms and conditions and limits. ADs can

provide forward/option contracts to FIIs with rupee as one of the currencies to such customers on the basis of their declaration of the market value of their entire investment in equity and/or debt in India as on a particular date. The cost of hedge is to be met out of repatriable funds and/or inward remittance through normal banking channel. If the hedge becomes naked, the hedge may be allowed to continue to the original maturity.

- **October 2003:** Earlier, entities with foreign direct investment in India had to approach the Reserve Bank for case by case approval to hedge their investment. This has now been delegated to ADs who may enter into forward/option contracts with residents outside India to hedge the foreign direct investments made in India subject to verification of the exposure in India. All foreign exchange derivative contracts permissible for a person resident outside India once cancelled, are not eligible to be rebooked.

16.6 Foreign Exchange Exposure Norms of Commercial Banks

With the objective of providing greater operational flexibility, banks were given freedom to fix their own open exchange position limit.

Depending upon the asset liability profile, dealing expertise and other relevant factors, authorised dealers (ADs) in foreign exchange were accorded freedom to fix their own gap limits for more efficient management of their assets and liabilities.

Foreign exchange exposure norms for banks authorised to deal in foreign exchange, i.e. authorised dealers (ADs) are set out below:

16.6.1 Positions and Gaps:

1. RBI has stipulated foreign exchange exposure limits in the form of net overnight open position limit (including gold) (OPL) and aggregate gap limit (AGL) for banks. The OPL and AGL are required to be approved by the RBI.
2. Boards of directors of ADs are required to frame an

appropriate policy and fix suitable limits for various treasury functions.

16.6.2 Investments in Overseas Markets:

1. ADs can undertake investments in overseas money market instruments (including any debt instrument whose life to maturity does not exceed one year as on the date of purchase) and/or debt instruments issued by a foreign state with a residual maturity of less than one year, up to the limits approved by their board of directors. The instruments, however, are to be rated at least as AA (-) by Standard & Poor's or Aa3 by Moody's. For the purpose of investments in debt instruments other than the money market instruments of any foreign state, the Boards of banks may lay down country ratings and country-wise limits separately, wherever necessary.
2. ADs may also invest the undeployed FCNR(B) funds in overseas markets in long-term fixed income securities provided the maturity of the securities invested in does not exceed the maturity of the underlying FCNR(B) deposits.
3. ADs can also invest surplus in *Nostro* accounts through overnight placement and investments with their overseas branches/correspondents subject to adherence to the gap limits approved by the RBI.

16.6.3 Overseas Foreign Currency Borrowings:

1. The aggregate limit for almost all categories of overseas foreign currency borrowings of ADs is placed at 25 percent of their unimpaired Tier I capital or US$ 10 million (or its equivalent), whichever is higher. Funds so raised may be used for purposes other than lending in foreign currency to constituents in India and repaid without reference to the RBI. As an exception to this rule, ADs are permitted to use borrowed funds as also foreign currency funds received through swaps for granting foreign currency loans for export credit subject to certain stipulations. Besides this, subordinated debt placed by head offices of foreign banks with their branches in India

as Tier II capital is also treated outside the above limit.

16.6.4 Gold Transactions:

1. Only banks authorised by the RBI can deal in gold. Such banks can enter into forward contracts in India for buying and selling gold with those banks which are authorised to import gold and with their constituents (exporters of gold products, jewellery manufacturers and trading houses) in respect of the underlying sale/purchase and loan transactions in gold with them. The tenor of such contracts, however, should not exceed six months.
2. Banks may use exchange-traded and over-the-counter hedging products available overseas to manage the price risk. However, while using products involving options, it needs to be ensured that there is no net receipt of premium, either direct or implied.

16.6.5 Vostro Accounts

1. The aggregate limit for temporary overdrawals in *vostro* account of overseas branches/correspondents is ₹ 5 crore in aggregate for meeting normal business requirements.

16.7 Present Structure of Foreign Exchange Market

The Indian market is not yet very deep and broad, and is characterised by uneven flow of demand and supply over different periods. The market is also characterised by a few major players, and lumpy public sector demands, particularly on account of payments for oil imports and servicing of public debt. In this situation, RBI has been prepared to make sales and purchases of foreign currency in order to even out lumpy demand and supply in the relatively thin foreign exchange market and to smoothen jerky movements. However, such interventions are not governed by a predetermined target or band around the exchange rate.

With the institution of the market determined exchange rate on March 1, 1993 and large capital inflows during 1993-95, RBI has undertaken several measures to widen and deepen the foreign exchange market. As on March 22, 2019, there were 99 banks under Category I, authorised to deal in foreign exchange, referred to as Authorised Dealers (ADs). Of these, most foreign banks and bigger Indian banks actively quote two-way prices. The banks deal among themselves directly or through the foreign exchange brokers.

Besides banks, term lending institutions have been given restricted dealing licences. Foreign Exchange Dealers Association of India (FEDAI) sets ground rules for fixation of commercial and other charges and involves itself in matters of mutual interest of ADs. The market trades freely in spot and forward exchange contracts, and to a limited extent in derivatives. The efficiency/liquidity of the market is often gauged in terms of bid/offer spreads. Wider spreads are an indication of an illiquid or a one-way market.

In India, the foreign exchange market is a three-level structure consisting of: (a) Reserve Bank of India (RBI) at the top, (b) authorised dealers licensed by the RBI, and (c) customers (exporters, importers, companies, and other foreign exchange earners). In addition to these main market players, there are foreign exchange money changers who bring buyers and sellers together, but are not permitted to deal in foreign exchange on their own account.

Dealings in the foreign exchange market include transactions between authorised dealers and the exporters/importers and other customers, transactions among authorised dealers themselves, transactions with overseas banks and transactions between authorised dealers and the RBI.

The mode of exchange rate determination is of paramount importance to the development of foreign exchange market. There is no single exchange rate regime which can be considered appropriate for all countries, at all times. Though the choice of an exchange rate regime is country-specific and contingent on macroeconomic policies, there is a growing consensus globally in favour of a flexible/floating rate regime.

16.7.1 Market Segments: The Indian foreign exchange market is a decentralised multiple dealership market comprising two segments—the spot and the derivatives market. In the spot market, currencies are traded at the prevailing rates and the settlement or value date is two business days ahead. The two-day period gives adequate time for the parties to send instructions to debit and credit the appropriate bank accounts at home and abroad.

The derivatives market encompasses forwards, swaps and options. Though forward contracts exist for maturities up to 1 year, majority of forward contracts are for 1 month, 3 months, or 6 months. Forward contracts for longer periods are not common because of the uncertainties involved and related pricing issues.

A swap transaction in the foreign exchange market is a combination of a spot and a forward in the opposite direction.

The spot market is the dominant segment of the Indian foreign exchange market. The derivative segment of the foreign exchange market is assuming significance and the activity in this segment is gradually rising.

16.7.2 Market Players: Players in the Indian foreign exchange market include: (a) authorised dealers (ADs), mostly banks who are authorised to deal in foreign exchange, (b) foreign exchange brokers who act as intermediaries, and (c) customers—individuals and corporates who need foreign exchange for their transactions. Though customers are major players in the foreign exchange market, for all practical purposes they depend upon ADs and brokers. In the spot foreign exchange market, foreign exchange transactions were earlier dominated by brokers. However, the situation has changed with the evolving market conditions and as of now the transactions are dominated by ADs. Brokers continue to dominate the derivatives market.

RBI intervenes in the market essentially to ensure orderly market conditions. The RBI undertakes sales/purchases of foreign currency in periods of excess demand/supply in the market.

Foreign Exchange Dealers' Association of India (FEDAI) plays a special role in the foreign exchange market for ensuring smooth and speedy growth of the foreign exchange market in all its aspects. All ADs are required to become members of the FEDAI and execute an undertaking to the effect that they would abide by the terms and conditions stipulated by the FEDAI for transacting foreign exchange business. The FEDAI is also the accrediting authority for the foreign exchange brokers in the inter-bank foreign exchange market.

The licences for ADs are issued to banks and other institutions, on their request, under Section 10(1) of the Foreign Exchange Management Act, 1999. ADs are divided into different categories.

All scheduled commercial banks—which include public sector banks, private sector banks and foreign banks operating in India—belong to category I of ADs.

All upgraded full-fledged money changers (FFMCs) and select regional rural banks (RRBs) and co-operative banks belong to category II of ADs.

Select financial institutions such as EXIM Bank belong to category III of ADs.

All merchant transactions in the foreign exchange market have to be necessarily undertaken directly through ADs. However, to provide depth and liquidity to the inter-bank segment, ADs have been permitted to utilise the services of brokers for better price discovery in their inter-bank transactions.

The customer segment of the foreign exchange market comprises major public sector units, corporates and business entities with foreign exchange exposure. It is generally dominated by select large public sector units such as Indian Oil Corporation (IOC), Oil and Natural Gas Commission (ONGC), Bharat Heavy Electrical Limited (BHEL), Steel Authority of India Limited (SAIL), Maruti Udyog and also the Government of India (for defence and civil debt service) as also big private sector corporates like Reliance Group, Tata Group and Larsen and Toubro, among others.

In recent years, foreign institutional investors (FIIs) have emerged as major players in the foreign exchange market.

16.8 Sources of Supply of and Demand for Dollars

16.8.1 From Where the Dollar Comes? The major sources of supply of dollars (foreign exchange) in India are as under:

- Receipts on account of exports of goods from India to other countries.
- Receipts on account of rendering of services (invisibles) like shipping, banking, software and insurance to other countries.
- Factor incomes (rent and interest) of resident Indians from their property and investments in other countries.
- Financial transfers like foreign remittances sent by Indian working abroad.
- Inflows in the capital account such as foreign direct investment (FDI), portfolio investment, external commercial borrowings (ECBs) and non-resident deposits.
- External aid received by the Government.

16.8.2 To Where the Dollar Goes? The demand for dollar emanates mainly from the following:

- Payments for goods imported from other countries.
- Payments for services received from other countries.
- Outflows on account of direct and portfolio investment.
- Redemption of NRI deposits.
- Aid by India to other countries

16.9 Derivative Market Instruments

Derivatives play a crucial role in developing the foreign exchange market as they enable market players to hedge against underlying exposures and shape the overall risk profile of participants in the market. Banks in India have been increasingly using derivatives for managing risks and have also been offering these products to corporates. In India, various informal forms of derivatives contracts have existed for a long time though the formal introduction of a variety of instruments in the foreign exchange derivatives market started only in the post-reform period, especially from mid-1990s. The foreign exchange derivative products that are now available in Indian financial markets can be grouped into three broad segments, viz. forwards, options (foreign currency rupee options and cross currency options) and currency swaps (foreign currency rupee swaps and cross currency swaps).

The most widely used derivative instruments are the forwards and foreign exchange swaps (rupee-dollar).

16.10 Foreign Exchange Dealers' Association of India

FEDAI was set up in August 1958 as a regulatory body, assuming at inception, primarily, the role of Exchange Banks' Association. The FEDAI members are all Authorised Dealers (Category I) in foreign exchange (101 members as in April 2019), who are required to be members of the FEDAI and abide by its rules and guidelines, as per licensing norms of Reserve Bank.

In the formative years, the FEDAI's principal preoccupation was ensuring a level playing field in the foreign exchange market domain in India, by laying down transaction-based guidelines, and transaction-based tariff norms for member banks. The FEDAI's role has subsequently evolved very substantially, with a facilitatory side also emerging strongly. While, with considerable deregulation in the market, the FEDAI dissociated completely from laying down tariff norms for the members from September 1999 onwards, there was a quantum jump in its advisory and facilitatory activities.

Guidelines and rules for forex business (other than prescription of tariff norms), continue to be among the FEDAI's main activities. These include announcement of several daily, weekly, monthly and quarterly market-related numbers, which are primarily used by member banks for revaluation of portfolio, mark-to-market exercise, quoting of rates in NRI deposits, etc., and are also available to the public at large for information.

Additionally, training of bank personnel in various areas of foreign exchange business, advising/assisting members in settling issues among themselves and dealings with customers, piloting of new products/innovations on behalf of members with regulators, representing member banks at Government/Reserve Bank/other bodies, representing members on International Chambers of Commerce (ICC)'s Commission on Banking Techniques and Practices, Paris (which inter alia frames rules like Uniform Customs and Practice for Documentary Credit (UCP 500–now superseded by UCP 600), accreditation of forex brokers, laying down a Code of Conduct between member banks and brokers, and closely monitoring market conduct are some of the other areas where the Association has become very active over the years. FEDAI now plays a catalytic role for smooth functioning of the market through close co-ordination with the Reserve Bank, sister organisations like FIMMDA, Forex Association of India and others.

To sum up, various reforms measures initiated have resulted in significant growth of the foreign exchange market. Also, despite liberalisation of capital account and introduction of market determined exchange rate, the foreign exchange market in India remained stable during the 1990s barring a few episodes of volatility. India's exchange rate policy of managing volatility without fixed target, while allowing the underlying demand and supply conditions to determine the exchange rate, has yielded satisfactory results. Various reforms measures in the foreign exchange market have also led to the widening and deepening of the forex market in India as reflected in the substantial increase in the foreign exchange market turnover, particularly in the inter-bank segment.

True, the reforms in the forex market have yielded good results, but there are some issues which need to be addressed to enhance its stability and ensure further growth. Although the turnover in the market increased considerably over the years, it still remains small. Since the market lacks depth, the RBI has to actively intervene in the market to absorb and provide liquidity. There is, therefore, need to take steps to further develop the market so that the need for intervention by the RBI is minimised.

Derivatives are an important instrument of risk hedging. Although a few derivative products have been introduced, there has not been much activity in some of them, such as FRAs. There is a need to further develop a range of derivative products like forex options.

The momentous developments over the past few years are reflected in the enhanced risk-bearing capacity of banks along with rising foreign exchange trading volumes and finer margins. The foreign exchange market has acquired depth. The conditions in the foreign exchange market have also generally remained orderly. While it is not possible for any country to remain completely unaffected by developments in international markets, India was able to keep the spill over effect of the Asian crisis to a minimum through constant monitoring and timely action, including recourse to strong monetary measures, when necessary. However, the recent global financial turmoil has triggered an increased volatility in the foreign exchange market. The Indian economy is moving towards fuller capital account convertibility, albeit in a calibrated manner.

With the economy moving towards fuller capital account convertibility in a calibrated manner, focused regulation and monitoring of the foreign exchange market assumes added importance. In this context, there is a need to strengthen infrastructure, transparency and disclosure, and product range in the foreign exchange derivative markets. Strengthening the trading infrastructure, market conduct, transparency of OTC derivatives in the foreign exchange market, accounting and disclosures in line with international practices, including disclosures by non-bank corporates, needs to be done on a priority basis. The recent introduction of currency futures is a step in this regard.

Bibliography

Acharya, Viral V., Hemal Khandwala and T. Sabri Öncü (2013), "The Growth of a Shadow Banking System in Emerging Markets: Evidence from India", *Journal of International Money and Finance*, 39, 207-230.

Basu, Priya (2005), "A Financial System for India's Poor", *Economic and Political Weekly*, No. 37.

Bhatt, Nitin and Y.S.P. Thorat (2001), "India's Regional Rural Banks: The Institutional Dimension of Reforms", *Journal of Microfinance*, Vol. 3, No. 1.

Chattopadhyay, S.K. (2010), "RBI Working Paper on Financial Inclusion in India: A Case Study of West Bengal", Working Paper Series, September, RBI.

Financial Action Task Force (FATF) (2013), "Anti-money Laundering and Terrorist Financing Measures and Financial Inclusion".

Fisher, Thomas and M.S. Sriram (2000), "Beyond Micro-credit: Putting Development Back into Micro-finance", Vistaar Publications.

Gopinath, S. (2005), "Recent Development in Forex, Money and Government Securities Markets: Account and Outlook", *RBI Bulletin*, August.

Government of India, Ministry of Finance, "Budget Papers" (various years).

—Ministry of Finance, "Economic Survey" (various issues).

Gupta, Sanjeev Kumar (2011), "Financial Inclusion: IT as Enabler", Reserve Bank of India Occasional Papers 31, No. 2.

International Monetary Fund, "Global Financial Stability Report", 2005.

Jadhav, Narendra (2003), "Central Bank Strategies, Credibility and Independence: Global Evolution and the Indian Experience", RBI Occasional Papers.

Jadhav, Narendra, Partha Ray, D. Bose and Indranil Sen Gupta (2003), "The Reserve Bank of India's Balance Sheet: Analytics and Dynamics of Evolution", RBI Occasional Papers.

Jalan, Bimal, "Finance and Development: Which Way Now?", *RBI Bulletin*, January 2001.

Johri and Jauhari (1994), "Role of Computers in Banking Operation

Systems", Himalaya Publishing House, New Delhi.

Kalpana, K. (2005), "Shifting Trajectories in Micro Finance Discourse", *Economic and Political Weekly*, Vol. XL, No. 51.

Kohli, S.S. (2001), "Indian Banking Industry: Emerging Challenges", *IBA Bulletin*, March.

Kulkarni, R.V. (2000), "Changing Face of Banking from Brick and Mortar Banking to E- Banking", *IBA Bulletin,* January.

Malhotra, R.N. (1990), "Evolution of Financial System", Nineteenth Frank Moraes Memorial Lecture, Chennai, September.

Merton, R.C. (2005), "Financial Innovation and Economic Performance", *Journal of Applied Corporate Finance*, Vol. 4, Issue 4, 12-22.

Mohan, Rakesh (2003), "Transforming Indian Banking: In Search of a Better Tomorrow", *RBI Bulletin.*

Nair, C.K.G. (2012), "Financial Sector Reforms: Refining the Architecture", in R. Malhotra (ed.), 'A Critical Decade: Policies for India's Development', Oxford University Press, New Delhi.

Puhazhendhi, V. and K.J.S. Satyasai (2001), "Microfinance for Rural People: An Impact Study", NABARD, Mumbai.

Rajan, R. and L. Zingales (1998), "Financial Dependence and Growth", *American Economic Review*, Vol. 88.

Rajaraman, Indira (2005), "Financing Rural Infrastructure in Developing Countries", *Applied Econometrics and International Development,* Vol. 5.

Rangarajan, C. (2008), "Report of the Committee of Financial Inclusion", Planning Commission, Government of India.

Rao, K.S. (2009), "Micro Credit Engine for Inclusive Growth", *The Indian Banker*, September, Vol. 4, No. 9, 40-43.

Reddy, Y.V. (1997), "Financial Sector Reforms and RBI's Balance Sheet Management", *RBI Bulletin*, December.

Reserve Bank of India, "Report of the Committee on Banking Sector Reforms (Chairman: M. Narasimham)", 1998.

——"Core Principles of Effective Banking Supervision", 1999.

——"Report of the Working Group on Internet Banking (Chairman: S.R. Mittal)", 2001.

——"Reserve Bank of India: Functions and Working", Reserve Bank Staff College, Chennai, 2001.

——"Report of the Working Group on Monitoring of Systemically Important Financial Intermediaries (Financial Conglomerates), 2004.

——"Report of the Technical Group on Money Market", May 2005.

——"Report of the Internal Technical Group on Central Government Securities Market", July 2005.

——"History of the Reserve Bank of India" (Volume III), 2005.

——"Banking Structure in India: The Way Forward", Discussion Paper, 2013.

——"Report on Currency and Finance" (various years).

——"Handbook of Statistics on Indian Economy" (various years).

——"Bulletins".

——"Occasional Papers".

——"Annual Report" (various issues).

Rajan, Raghuram (2009), "A Hundred Small Steps: Report of the Committee on Financial Sector Reforms", Planning Commission, Government of India, Sage Publications, New Delhi.

Sarangi, Umesh Chandra (2010), "Report of the Task Force on Credit Related Issues of Farmers", Ministry of Agriculture, Government of India.

Sarkar, A.N. and Jagjit Singh (2006), "Savings-led Micro Finance to Bank the Unbankables: Sharing of Global Experience", *Global Economic Review*, July, Vol. 7, No. 2.

Sarma, M. (2008), "Index of Financial Inclusion", ICRIER Working Paper, August.

Shetty, S.L. (2003), "Credit Flows to Rural Poor", mimeo, EPW Research Foundation, Mumbai.

Sinha, Saurabh (1998), "Micro Credit: Impact, Training and Sustainability", Institute of Development Studies (IDS), Vol. 29, No. 4, October, University Sussex, U.K.

Srikrishna, B.N. (2013), "Report of the Financial Sector Legislative Reforms Commission", Volume I, Ministry of Finance, Government of India.

Srinivasan, N. (2012), "Microfinance India: State of the Sector Report 2011", Sage Publications, New Delhi.

Tarapore, S.S. (1990), "Domestic Debt Management Policy and Monetary Control", 18th SEANZA Central Banking Course Lectures, Reserve Bank of India, Mumbai.

——(1996), "The Government Securities Market: The Next Stage of Reform", Valedictory Address at the Conference on Government Securities Market, Securities Trading Corporation of India, April.

Tara, S. Nair (2005), "The Transforming World of Indian Micro Finance", *Economic and Political Weekly*, April 23.

Thingalaya, N.K. (2000), "The Other Side of Rural Banking", BIRD Publication, Lucknow.

Thorat, U. (2010), Keynote address at a panel session on "Setting New Paradigm in Regulation" at the FICCI-IBA Conference on 'Global Banking: Paradigm Shift'.

—(2002), "Developing Bond Markets to Diversify Long-Term Development Finance: Country Study of India", *Asia-Pacific Development Journal*, June.

Thorat, Y.S.P. (2011), "Report of the Working Group on Outreach of Institutional Finance, Co-operatives, and Risk Management", Planning Commission, Government of India.

Trivedi, Pratima (2008), "Financial Inclusion: A Must for Financial Stability", *Vinimaya*, Vol. XXIX (2), 59-64.

Umapathy, Deeptha, Parul Agarwal and Santadarshan Sadhu (2012), "A Scoping Study of Financial Literacy Training Programmes in India".

UNCDF (2006), "Building Inclusive Financial Sectors for Development", UNCDF, May.

Valpy, FitzGerald (2006), "Financial Development and Economic Growth: A Critical View", Background paper for World Economic and Social Survey, 2006, Oxford University, U.K.

World Bank, "Improving Access to Finance for India's Rural Poor", The World Bank, 2008.

—"Measuring Financial Inclusion", Policy Research Working Paper, 6025, World Bank, Washington D.C., 2011.

—"Financial Access: The State of Financial Inclusion through the Crisis", Consultative Group to Assist the Poor (CGAP), 2010.

Websites

Ministry of Finance, Government of India

Ministry of Corporate Affairs, Government of India

Reserve Bank of India (RBI)

Securities and Exchange Board of India (SEBI)

Niti Aayog

World Bank

Index

Index